HOW TO TREAT ADDICTION?

Aharon Shabi
How to treat addiction?

Literary Editing: Gili Tal-Oren

Published by Spines
ISBN: 979-8-89691-989-6

Spines

HOW TO TREAT ADDICTION?

EFT

CHANGING EMOTIONS - CHANGING BEHAVIOR

AHARON SHABI

CONTENTS

"In my early years as a therapist, I asked myself: How should I treat? How can I heal? How can I help my clients change? Today, I would frame the question differently: How can I create a relationship that fosters my clients' growth and development?" —Carl Rogers.

To Smadar, Ido, Bar, and Roy

INTRODUCTION

Finally, there was someone who truly knew me and believed in me. My sessions with my therapist became a safe space, a home. There was a genuine connection—real, positive, understanding, and loving. She was caring, and attentive, and saw me for who I truly was. She rejoiced in my happiness and shared my sorrow when I was in pain.
–Betty, a patient

Betty, who struggled with addiction, captured in just a few sentences the essence of the relationship she had with her therapist. This interpersonal therapeutic relationship provided her with security, love, and a renewed sense of self-worth, which became the foundation for her journey to overcoming addiction. The subject of this book, Emotion-Focused Therapy for Addiction, is a therapeutic approach designed to transform painful and maladaptive emotions—such as anxiety and depression, often rooted in trauma, neglect, or harm—into more adaptive, empowering feelings like self-worth and strength. This process facilitates the creation of a new personal narrative and emotional transformation, leading to meaningful behavioral change. Betty's prolonged use of psychoactive substances, including drugs, medication, and alcohol, led to deep dependence and psychological, emotional, and physical changes that severely impaired her functioning, both short- and long-term. The emotion-focused therapy she underwent provided her with a corrective emotional experience, allowing her to reclaim feelings of pride and self-worth.

The misuse of psychoactive substances and addiction to them cause significant mental health issues, including symptoms of anxiety, depression, and loss of control. Addiction is defined in the DSM-5, the diagnostic manual of the American Psychiatric Association, as a disorder characterized by a maladaptive pattern causing clinical distress. People struggling with long-term addiction often experience intense, uncontrollable emotions, such as depression, shame, and sorrow. These feelings often stem from experiences of rejection, abuse, and humiliation—some conscious, others unconscious. Excessive substance use is sometimes an attempt to "solve" deep-seated emotional pain, but in practice, it burdens users' lives. For many, addictive behavior becomes a cycle of anxiety, fear, risk, and hopelessness.

The goal of this book is to explore how emotion-focused therapy can serve as an effective tool for addressing addiction, raising questions such as:

- Can emotional transformation provide a corrective experience for patients struggling with addiction?
- What methods can bring about significant change for patients who find it difficult to express their emotions?
- Is it possible to help patients who have experienced abuse, harm, and trauma to regulate

and process intense emotions in the context of addiction treatment?
- What constitutes effective treatment for addiction?

These questions will be addressed through the lens of Emotion-Focused Therapy (EFT), based on humanistic psychology and the pioneering work of Les Greenberg. The EFT approach centers on transforming maladaptive emotions, such as anxiety and shame, into positive, transformative emotions like self-worth and a sense of capability. The therapy aims to integrate these new emotions into the emotional system, leading to functional and behavioral changes. Key components of the intervention process include:

- Enhancing emotional awareness: Identifying unresolved emotions and addressing them.
- Processing memories of core pain: Creating space for emotions and memories tied to traumatic experiences.
- Strengthening emotional expression: Developing the ability to express emotions in a healthy, adaptive manner.
- Physical inner focus: Cultivating awareness of the connection between the body and emotions.
- Regulating and processing emotions: Balancing the turbulent emotional system.
- Processing emotions related to attachment figures: Addressing complex emotions tied to significant past and present relationships.

The foundation of emotional change in Emotion-Focused Therapy (EFT) lies in establishing strong therapeutic interpersonal relationships, built on a solid alliance between the therapist and the client. In such relationships, support, containment, and empathy are key elements. Recent studies have highlighted the positive impact of EFT on individuals coping with complex trauma, depression, anxiety, and relational and family challenges.

The research presented in this book explores how this approach can benefit another population—individuals struggling with addiction. The study was conducted in an outpatient addiction treatment setting in Israel, combining emotional therapy with additional psychosocial methods. Findings indicate that emotion-focused practices enhanced participants' sense of security and self-efficacy, helped them adapt to the therapeutic framework, and supported their commitment to abstaining from substance abuse. Recovery from addiction is a long and complex process, especially among populations that are less likely to engage in the treatment, tend to drop out early and face stigma, exclusion, and feelings of hopelessness in their daily lives. This book emphasizes the need for precise and tailored treatment for this population, where processing early maladaptive emotional experiences and developing emotional coping skills are central. This approach not only offers a corrective emotional experience but also opens the door to significant behavioral change and improvement in patients' quality of life.

Les Greenberg developed a typology of six categories for emotion-focused interpersonal therapy:

1. Enhancing Emotional Awareness: Helping the client identify and connect with suppressed emotions.
2. Emotional Expression: Encouraging the client to express their emotions.
3. Emotional Regulation: Reducing the intensity of overwhelming emotions to allow for their processing, transformation, and the attainment of a sense of control.
4. Emotional Reflection: Reflecting on emotions and deepening understanding to create a new narrative and perspective.
5. Emotional Transformation: Transforming maladaptive emotions, such as shame, into empowering emotions, like self-worth, and integrating them into the client's emotional system. This process involves identifying positive emotions, evaluating their relevance, and assessing their alignment with the client's current emotional state.
6. Corrective Emotional Experience: Facilitating change within the therapeutic relationship by transforming maladaptive emotions, such as anger, into adaptive ones, such as a sense of control.

The research underlying this book proposes extending emotion-focused therapy (EFT) to individuals struggling with addiction, based on two central themes:

1. Increasing Emotional Awareness and Mapping Maladaptive Emotions:
    - Strengthening the client's ability to identify maladaptive emotions and understand their origins (e.g., rejection, deprivation, trauma).
    - Examining how maladaptive interpretations perpetuate addiction.
2. Promoting Proactivity and Emotional Management:
    - Encouraging the client to experience emotions in the "here and now" within the therapeutic relationship, while observing them from a new perspective and reassessing their relevance to the client's current reality.
    - Creating alternative interpretations of maladaptive emotions and transforming them —for example, converting emotions like shame into positive feelings such as confidence, strength, and control—to facilitate functional changes, reduce substance use, and even achieve abstinence.

A longitudinal quantitative and qualitative study that was conducted in an outpatient addiction treatment setting in Israel, examining the impact of individualized emotional therapy on clients dealing with addiction, found that the interpersonal therapeutic components applied to 36 clients had a significant contribution. These clients developed awareness of their emotions and maladaptive behaviors, successfully transforming them into positive emotions such as confidence and self-efficacy, which led to significant behavioral changes, including abstinence from drugs and alcohol for up to eight months. However, the study also identified several challenges in applying this method, such as difficulties in establishing therapeutic relationships with some clients, therapists' struggles in helping clients regulate intense emotions, and challenges in facilitating emotional transformation processes. To address these challenges, therapists emphasized interpersonal processes, focusing on supportive and empathetic communication, strengthening clients' capacity for self-compassion, and constructing a new emotional narrative based on self-worth and security. These strategies align with findings from existing research. Effective emotion-focused therapy for populations dealing with addiction requires combining emotional and practical interventions. This includes support in exercising rights, integrating into employment and housing, resolving family issues, advocacy, and personal support. Such actions could help remove daily barriers and enhance clients' willingness to engage in therapy.

Throughout this book, case studies and excerpts from emotion-focused interpersonal therapy sessions with clients struggling with addiction will be presented, alongside additional case studies from the research literature. To protect clients' privacy, their identifying details have been altered. Quotes from theorists and thinkers throughout the book were sourced from publicly available online materials.

Structure of the Book

The book is divided into ten chapters, each focusing on a different aspect of addiction and emotion-focused interpersonal therapy:

• Chapter 1 explores addiction to psychoactive substances, covering substance dependence, the characteristics of substance use, profiles of populations along the addiction spectrum, and the use of substances for self-healing.

• Chapter 2 discusses current therapeutic practices and intervention methods in addiction treatment, as well as the central challenges faced by individuals struggling with addiction.

• Chapter 3 outlines the features of interpersonal therapy and the path toward mental health and well-being, including the therapeutic journey, overcoming treatment barriers, and providing unconditional support to clients dealing with addiction.

• Chapter 4 introduces emotion-focused interpersonal therapy and its foundational theory, examining the human emotional system, the impact of trauma on emotions, and the innovation of transforming maladaptive emotions into constructive ones.

• Chapter 5 addresses the clinical tasks in emotion-focused therapy.

• Chapter 6 explores practical processes related to emotional transformation in short-term therapy, detailing how maladaptive emotions can be converted into more empowering ones and what constitutes a corrective emotional experience.

• Chapter 7 focuses on integrating emotion-focused therapy with harm reduction in addiction treatment, examining ethical challenges and methods of addressing them.

• Chapter 8 discusses emotion-focused therapy in the digital space, particularly in the aftermath of the COVID-19 pandemic, and outlines necessary adaptations for online therapy while maintaining core principles of interpersonal therapy and empathy.

• Chapter 9 offers solutions to challenges in emotion-focused therapy, with an emphasis on the strength and quality of therapeutic relationships.

• Chapter 10 is the conclusion, exploring the practical application of the interpersonal approach with clients in severe distress and how to motivate them to embrace emotional change.

This book is informed by research on emotion-focused interpersonal therapy, a study conducted among populations on the addiction spectrum, and my experience as a psychosocial practitioner and manager in both public and private systems. Over the years, I have provided therapy to adolescents and adults in severe distress, struggling with frustration, anxiety, and sadness arising from emotional and behavioral challenges. My therapeutic approach emphasized emotional interpersonal dialogue, empathy, and containment, aiming to promote self-acceptance and personal growth. Additionally, my experience as an academic lecturer in education, criminology, and social work in Israel, as well as my publications in professional journals, has deepened my understanding of therapeutic emotional content, which is reflected in this book. This book is intended for practitioners working with at-risk populations, especially those struggling with addiction, as well as readers interested in addiction and potential therapeutic approaches to address this complex phenomenon.

I hope that this book provides an in-depth introduction to both the world of addiction and the framework of emotion-focused therapy, inspiring professionals across various fields to apply this method in practice. This approach could offer marginalized populations an authentic opportunity for growth, healing, and a better future.

Dr. Aharon Shabi

1

WHAT IS ADDICTION? CHARACTERISTICS OF THE PHENOMENON AND ITS TYPES

Mike is a twenty-nine-year-old single man who lives in a shared apartment and has not worked for the past ten months. He was referred by his family doctor to a center for addiction treatment due to his intensive use of cannabis and alcohol. In a conversation with the therapist, he mentions that he has been using these substances for about ten years, but in the past two years, he feels he has lost control over the quantity and frequency of his usage. In the past, he tried to quit using drugs but failed in his attempts. As a result of his excessive use of cannabis and alcohol, there is tension between him and his parents. During the introductory meetings with the therapist, Mike appears embarrassed and ashamed that he has found himself in a treatment center once again. He finds it hard to believe that stopping substance use will help resolve other difficulties he is experiencing in his life.

"I have to say, I feel calm when I'm using the drug," he says, his eyes fixed on the corner of the room. "My thoughts fall into place, and thanks to the substances, I've been able to create social connections. I don't understand why I need treatment."

The therapist leans forward, her gaze soft. "From what you're describing," she says, "cannabis has become a part of your life. You're saying you don't see a reason to stop using it, even though your family doctor mentioned he is concerned about you and believes that excessive substance use is significantly harming your health and daily functioning. You mentioned that recently you've been experiencing dizziness, depression, and a sense of disconnection. I feel that the use of drugs and alcohol isn't just bringing you benefits, and as you described, it isn't really helping alleviate the pain you're feeling—especially in recent months due to the conflict with your parents over substance use and your unemployment. I sense that the failure you experienced when you tried to quit the substances a few months ago left you disappointed and pessimistic, and maybe that's contributed to the feeling that there's no point in putting effort into that direction. Am I being accurate?"

"To be honest," Mike shrugs, "I don't have much patience for talks and discussions. I've been in therapy before and nothing changed. Yes, I have problems that cannabis and alcohol don't solve, but at least these substances help me disconnect. That's something. I honestly don't know what to do."

The therapist nods understandingly and watches him for a long moment. "The fact that you're coming to our meetings and sharing with me the difficult experiences you've been having over the past few years, particularly the loneliness stemming from disconnecting from your family, allows me to hear another voice within you, one that still wants to understand what led to the current situation and how we can change the feelings of anxiety and sadness you're experiencing these days. I believe that together we can approach the obstacles you face differently. The fact that you've returned to treatment is an opportunity to address the challenges you're describing in a new way and, over time, create change. I'm with you."

Mike finds himself at a dead end, both when it comes to breaking the cycle of substance abuse (Shabi, 2021), and in understanding the reasons for his dependence on cannabis and how to escape the difficulties of daily life. So, what is this closed cycle in the context of addiction to substances? And what are the possible solutions for populations dealing with Difficulty and Distress? This chapter will discuss the characteristics of substance use, the traits of populations that use substances, the meaning of the term "self-healing," which explains the background of the closed cycle in the field of addiction, and the intervention processes currently taking place within these populations.

Addictive Substances: Basic Assumptions

The symptoms of addiction and its various manifestations appear in an individual on psychological, physiological, and behavioral levels, and arise from a shared biopsychosocial etiology (NIDA, 2018). There is broad agreement in the field of research that individuals who excessively use psychoactive substances, including drugs, alcohol, and medications, invest a great deal of time thinking about the substances and engaging with them, often struggling to stop using. Substance abuse often begins in adolescence or early adulthood and is characterized by periods of use followed by periods of exacerbation throughout life. For some people, substance use continues for years despite the negative consequences and harm caused by the use (Monezi & Micheli, 2016). A person dealing with addiction to substances experiences cravings for the psychoactive substance, becomes anxious when unable to obtain it, and feels they are losing control. Some people may replace the use of psychoactive substances with other addictive behaviors (Monezi & Micheli, 2016).

Etiology

The biopsychosocial risk factors that contribute to the development of dependency on psychoactive substances arise from the characteristics of the substance itself, the personal characteristics of the user, and the environment in which they live (NIDA, 2014). Genetic factors and epigenetic inheritance account for 40%–60% of the factors leading to substance dependence, alongside environmental influences, psychological difficulties, and medical issues. According to the U.S. National Institute on Drug Abuse, individuals dealing with mental disorders and related diseases are at a higher risk of long-term use of psychoactive substances compared to other populations (NIDA, 2014). There is variability between addictive substances in their physiological and psychological effects. Currently, about one hundred substances are recognized as leading to addiction or significantly influencing mental and physiological states, including substances that depress the nervous system, stimulants, and hallucinogens (Reid, 2016). It's important to note that the list of illegal drugs is frequently updated and includes new synthetic drugs illegally produced in labs around the world. Below is a table outlining the types of substances commonly used and their known physiological and psychological effects.

Psychological and physiological effects	Examples	Type of drug
A feeling of heaviness, depression, difficulty in thinking, impaired understanding, poor judgment, hostile thoughts, suicidal thoughts.	Sedatives, sleeping pills, alcohol, benzodiazepines.	Drugs that depress the nervous system.
A decrease in heart rate, sweating, pupil constriction, reduced pain sensation, creation of a feeling of relaxation, dizziness, sleep disturbances, nausea, and euphoria (during repeated use).	Painkillers: codeine, opium, morphine, heroin, synthetic narcotics – methadone.	
Release of inhibitions, feelings of drowsiness and indifference, decreased concentration, distortion of time perception, changes in sensory perception, increased heart rate, paranoid thoughts, psychotic disturbances, schizophrenia, anxiety, disorientation, mood swings.	Cannabis: marijuana, hashish, grass, joint, diras.	
Relief of chronic pain, antiemetic, anti-nausea, improves symptoms during medical treatments.	Medical cannabis.	
Increased metabolism rate in the body, elevated blood pressure and heart rate, improved mood, a feeling of energy, episodic effects – schizophrenia and psychotic episodes.	Ecstasy, cocaine, amphetamines.	Drugs that stimulate the nervous system.
Increased alertness, a sense of self-confidence, euphoria.	MDMA.	
Dizziness, hot flashes or chills, mood swings, visual hallucinations, feeling of detachment from oneself, feeling of being persecuted, distortion of time perception.	LSD, mescaline, hallucinogenic mushrooms, ketamine.	Hallucinogenic drugs.

Psycho-Pharmacology

Numerous studies focus on the effects of psychoactive substances on the human body, particularly on the nervous system (Wampold, 2009). Understanding the pathways of psychoactive substances in the body helps explain their physiological and psychological effects. When a psychoactive substance is consumed through ingestion, smoking, or injection, it passes through the bloodstream or digestive system and reaches the synapses in the brain. These synapses are the gaps between brain cells, specifically between an axon fiber and a nerve cell or between a dendrite fiber and another nerve cell (Wampold, 2009). From the synapses, the substance reaches receptors where neurotransmitters are found, such as dopamine, serotonin, glutamate, and GABA. For example, dopamine, which is a mediator of reward and pleasure, is activated by the psychoactive substance and induces feelings of euphoria and relaxation. This feeling typically lasts only a very short time, and as the substance leaves the body, there is a decrease in receptor sensitivity to dopamine and a reduction in the sensation of euphoria. This condition can trigger frustration in the user and a desire to consume the substance again to recreate the positive feeling. When repeated consumption does not provide the expected pleasure due to the development of tolerance, a higher dosage of the substance is required to achieve the original effect.

This process leads to a closed cycle of substance use, characterized by repeated attempts and difficulty in stopping the use, the combination of additional substances, and poor daily functioning accompanied by feelings of frustration. This cycle creates severe and unbearable distress among adolescents, young adults, and adults.

How Did It All Begin?

The Use of Psychoactive Substances

The first psychoactive substances used by humans were tobacco and alcohol. Since the early seventeenth century, the use of marijuana and cannabis expanded, and by the end of the nineteenth century, opium use began, initially for medical purposes and later also for recreational use. In 1848, the U.S. government compiled a list of substances approved for medical use only and banned their recreational use. About seventy years later, in 1920, alcohol use was prohibited in the United States for thirteen years (Ichot & Smock, 2009). The religious establishment, both in the past and today, views the use of psychoactive substances for recreational purposes as sinful and supports the prohibitions imposed by various governments on the use of these substances. In the twentieth century, countries continued to impose restrictions and bans on non-medical use of drugs, though the prohibitions did not cover all substances. For example, heroin, LSD, and cannabis were permitted for use in some countries until the mid-twentieth century (Ichot & Smock, 2009). In the 1980s, there was a significant increase in the illegal production of drugs, particularly those referred to as "club drugs" such as ECSTASY and MDMA, and it was found that the public consuming these substances was growing. The legalization of cannabis in many Western countries, particularly from the 2000s onward, as well as the increased prescription of opioid medications by the medical establishment, have significantly contributed to the rise in psychoactive substance use and, consequently, to widespread functional problems among many populations (NIDA, 2018).

The first therapeutic model for addictions was developed in the 1930s in the United States by a group of individuals who excessively consumed alcohol. The group, which called itself "Alcoholics Anonymous" (A.A.), aimed to raise social awareness that excessive alcohol use is a chronic disease that the individual cannot control and that requires medical intervention (Ichot & Smock, 2009). The group worked to initiate social, political, and medical processes to gain recognition for institutional and medical treatment of the issue while promoting the concept of self-help as a way to cope with alcoholism. The group members developed a group framework based on the "12-step" method (Ronel, 2020), which relies on collective coping with addiction within a group framework, aimed at promoting self-control and personal empowerment. This self-help method is still applied today, not only in relation to excessive alcohol consumption, but also in other addiction areas such as drugs, gambling, and other addictive behaviors. It relies on total avoidance of the psychoactive substance or addictive behavior, and according to this method, the abandonment of the desire to control everything that is uncontrollable.

Most countries around the world, particularly Western nations, have developed over time policies in the field of addiction treatment, leading to the integration of formal medical and psychosocial treatments for this issue. In the 1980s, the bio-psycho-social model was developed, which today serves as the basis for therapeutic work in the addiction field. This model emphasizes the need for a comprehensive diagnosis of the addiction problem and the provision of treatment that combines biological, psychological, and social aspects. It also focuses on strengthening the psychological strengths of people coping with addiction, aiming to help them achieve emotional, cognitive, and behavioral changes that will allow them to reduce dependence on psychoactive substances and their addictive behaviors—and sometimes even stop them completely.

Gambling Behavior

During the 20th century, the understanding emerged that addictive behavior is not limited to the excessive use of psychoactive substances, but also manifests in the field of gambling. Gambling addiction shares similar characteristics with substance addiction and includes uncontrolled participation in various forms of gambling, both legal and illegal, including sports betting, casino games, card games, lottery, various raffles, and slot machines. The activity can be individual or social, in-person or online, occasional or regular. What defines the level of addiction the individual experiences are the frequency of this activity and the amount of time dedicated to it (Busfield, 2017). Similar to substance addiction, many countries around the world have begun to develop policies and intervention programs for gambling addiction. Studies indicate that gambling addiction shares similarities with substance addiction in several aspects, an uncontrollable urge to engage in the behavior and the perception of addiction as a means of self-healing. In light of this, the intervention and treatment methods recommended for both types of addictions —psychosocial and medical—carry similar characteristics. In the DSM-5 psychiatric diagnoses (2013), gambling behavior is defined as an addiction disorder, similar to substance use disorder. This definition includes extensive engagement in gambling, a lack of control over this behavior, impairment in daily functioning, and damage to the family and social environment. However, other addictive behaviors, such as addiction to sex, shopping, the internet, and gaming, are not yet defined as addiction disorders, as further research is needed to include them under this category. Similar to the urge for psychoactive substance use, social, biological, and psychological factors underlie the development of gambling behavior (Yau & Potenza, 2015). This disorder is manifested, among other things, by psychological withdrawal symptoms such as restlessness and anxiety when the person refrains from gambling. Additionally, tolerance develops, which is reflected in the increasing amount of time dedicated to gambling activities, in order to recreate the euphoric feeling the person experienced during the initial gambling activities.

People suffering from gambling disorder may attempt, often unsuccessfully, to reduce the amount of time devoted to this activity, but in many cases, they gradually lose interest in other areas that were once central to their lives. The focus on gambling persists despite the person experiencing psychosocial difficulties, sometimes against the backdrop of attempts to hide from family members and their environment the extent of their involvement in the activity and the financial losses involved. A significant factor influencing gambling behavior is the social environment. The existence of gambling activities among family members or friends in the community, as well as access to gambling venues, such as legal outlets authorized to operate lottery games, may exacerbate gambling behavior and make it more difficult for the person to reduce it. Studies examining the characteristics of individuals who regularly gamble indicate that 40% of them participate in illegal activities aimed at "generating income," such as theft, fraud, and money laundering, although most of these offenses are not violent (Petry et al., 2013). It was also found that individuals who use psychoactive substances and those with gambling behavior experience similar cognitive and emotional difficulties, which manifest in compulsiveness, impaired decision-making processes, and maladaptive thought and emotional patterns.

The prevalence of gambling behavior is particularly high among men and young people, and the risk of this addiction increases following early exposure to gambling, high availability of gambling games (which are now mainly conducted in the digital space), and a family history of addiction. Additionally, ethnic minority groups are at increased risk due to the associated challenges of immigration, such as unemployment and social and cultural barriers.

In conclusion, gambling behavior is linked to personal, familial, social, and environmental factors and is manifested in risky decision-making, maladaptive thinking patterns, a willingness to spend large amounts of money in a short period of time, a constant search for thrills, and persistence in the behavior despite the emotional, social, familial, and economic damage it causes. Similar to individuals who use psychoactive substances, individuals with gambling behavior require comprehensive psychosocial and medical treatment, aimed at alleviating emotional distress and helping to change emotional, cognitive, and behavioral patterns.

The Phenomenon of Addiction: Data

The phenomenon of substance abuse and addiction is widespread in Israel (Ministry of Welfare, 2019) and around the world (WHO, 2018). According to the OECD's annual report, approximately 5.6% of the global population (275 million people out of about 4.5 billion aged 15–61) reported using drugs. Of these, 9% (31 million people) suffered from "substance use disorder." It is worth noting that only one out of six individuals dealing with this disorder receives appropriate treatment (UNODC, 2018).

According to the World Health Organization (WHO, 2018), 43% of the global population aged 15 and above consumed alcohol, with a global average consumption of 6.4 liters per year per person. Additionally, 5.3% of global deaths are caused by harmful alcohol consumption, with the percentage of deaths involving alcohol rising to 13.5% in the age group 20–39.

Estimates regarding gambling addiction indicate that the rate of problematic gamblers ranges from 0.12% to 5.8% of the general population (Calado & Griffiths, 2016).

In Israel, according to data from the National Authority for the War on Drugs and Alcohol from 2016, there was an increase in the use of psychoactive substances among people aged 18–65 compared to the previous decade (Azari & Harel Fish, 2017).

The main findings are:

• 27% reported using cannabis.

• 2% reported using other illegal drugs.

• 29% reported being intoxicated at least once in the past year.

Regarding gambling in Israel, the 8th epidemiological survey by the National Authority for the War on Drugs and Alcohol found that among adults aged 18–65, approximately 5.7% reported frequent gambling (Azari & Harel Fish, 2017). Additionally, a survey conducted under the auspices of the lottery game system in 2018 found that 39% of the population participates in lotteries and gambling and of these:

• 3.5% were categorized as having a medium risk of developing an addiction.

• 2% were categorized as having a high risk of developing an addiction (Mifal HaPais Survey, 2018).

Substance Use and Behavior: Self-Medication

"The attempt to escape pain often creates additional pain" (Gabor Maté).

Why does the phenomenon of excessive substance use and addictive behavior not diminish, despite the heavy psychological and health costs it imposes? One possible answer to this question is that substance use is perceived by some in the public as a form of self-medication, intended to help the user cope with feelings such as anxiety, despair, insecurity, and the need for self-regulation and maintaining a sense of self-worth (DSM-5, 2013; Khantzian, 2013). The difficulties experienced by this population often stem from unresolved traumatic experiences, such as feelings of neglect, rejection, harm, or humiliation (Ehlers & Clark, 2000). However, it is important to emphasize that Self-medication is illusory: It provides relief, but only temporarily, and ultimately creates a vicious cycle of increasing difficulty and distress (Ettner et al., 2006).

Acute Trauma and Addictions

Experiences of harm and trauma are a significant factor in excessive substance use, as many users view these substances as a solution to the emotional difficulties they experience (APA, 2000). Acute traumas, which often result from loss, emotional deprivation, or sexual and physical abuse, deeply affect a person's sense of security and may lead to anxiety, despair, and withdrawal (McFarlane & Yehuda, 1996). Trauma causes the victims to disconnect from their sources of security, whether those are people, places, or areas that were meaningful to them in the past. This process leads to feelings of social and emotional isolation (Ehlers & Clark, 2000) and to an experience of life that is accompanied by shame, loss, and despair. In response to these feelings, many turn to alcohol, sedative medications, and pain relievers (opiates) in an attempt to avoid traumatic memories and experience temporary emotional relief (APA, 2000). However, this relief is deceptive and ultimately leads to a cycle of addiction, where the difficulty, insecurity, and despair only intensify (The Israeli Center for Addiction, 2023).

Populations on the Addiction Continuum

Adolescents

The research literature on adolescents within the addiction continuum indicates that not all adolescents who experiment with drugs and alcohol will develop severe problems or dysfunction (Zimmer & Boni-Nach, 2014). Drug and alcohol use among adolescents does not necessarily indicate pathology and may sometimes reflect part of the social norm of adolescence, including new experiences and dealing with risks. In other words, experimenting with substances is, to some extent, part of the process of achieving developmental goals characteristic of this age. However, gambling behavior or intensive substance use can lead to functional difficulties and a quick entry into the addiction cycle (Gabriel-Fried, Rehav

& Teichman, 2010). This stage, characterized by substance abuse and addictive behavior, may include difficulties in personal functioning within the family, school, and social systems. Some adolescents begin using substances or become addicted to gambling due to social and cultural influences, imitating their peer group. Some have difficulty understanding the significance and consequences of their behavior, both in the short and long term. The phenomenon of gambling addiction among adolescents is on the rise both globally and in Israel (Gabriel-Fried, 2023), including online gambling and gaming, an uncontrollable urge to return to gambling despite clear risks, and negative consequences such as academic difficulties and a sense of loss of control.

The gambling patterns of adolescents in Israel are similar to those in other countries. It has been found that boys gamble more frequently than girls. Additionally, some of the adolescents who gamble are children of gambling parents, and the age at which adolescents start gambling negatively affects their gambling behavior later on (Gabriel-Fried, Rehav & Teichman, 2010).

Educational and non-formal frameworks implement prevention programs aimed at reducing substance use and addictive behaviors among adolescents, but their success is only partial. There is a need for prevention programs that encourage adolescents to take initiative and engage in alternative activities, such as sports or other activities, in place of substance use, as well as the development of a dedicated treatment system for addictions at a young age. The increase in substance use and gambling addiction among adolescents requires more effective interventions that focus both on preventing addictive behaviors and on increasing emotional and social support for those struggling with addiction.

Women

Addiction to drugs and alcohol among women often develops at a young age, with some being mothers of young children. These women face significant personal, functional, and economic difficulties, and often struggle to maintain steady employment. Unlike men, most women on the addiction continuum are not involved in criminal or socially unacceptable activities. Another distinguishing feature is the use of legal substances such as alcohol, prescription drugs, and stimulants (Thom, 2010). Research shows that similar to men, women tend to use psychoactive substances as part of a "self-medication" mechanism, in order to cope with post-traumatic symptoms resulting from experiences of sexual or physical abuse, either in the past or currently. Among some women, there is a correlation between substance use and involvement in prostitution, where substance use is aimed at helping them cope with the emotional pain and suffering related to this behavior. Furthermore, women who use substances often suffer from additional psychiatric symptoms, such as anxiety, depression, and eating disorders (Thom, 2010).

Addiction among women carries unique characteristics, stemming from social, psychological, and trauma-related influences. Therefore, support and treatment programs should be based on the specific needs of this population to help them cope with the challenges of addiction and improve their quality of life.

Co-occurring Disorders

Co-occurring disorders, also known as dual diagnosis, refer to the situation where an individual simultaneously faces both a substance use disorder or addictive behavior and a mental health disorder. The connection between these disorders can arise from a variety of factors: genetic, neurobiological, psychological, social, environmental, and cultural. Similar to the general population, individuals suffering from mental health disorders sometimes use psychoactive substances as a self-medication strategy. These substances may temporarily alleviate symptoms of the disorder, but they ultimately "cover-up" the disorder and delay appropriate treatment intervention (Wamel et al., 2021). Long-term use of psychoactive substances, on the other hand, prolonged use of psychoactive substances by itself may lead to the emergence of a mental disorder, where the substance use and the mental state affect each other reciprocally.

People dealing with co-occurring disorders often experience mood swings, psychotic episodes, anxiety, and depression. Many of the affected individuals experience the onset of mental illness at a young age, and in 75% of cases, the mental disorder precedes the addiction. Research shows that most individuals with co-occurring disorders are men who struggle to escape risky situations and stop using substances. Their condition may lead to life-threatening risks due to difficulties with daily functioning and maintaining mental balance. One of the main challenges among this population is the lack of consistency in treatment, including sporadic medication intake and not following medical guidelines, which leads to repeated psychiatric hospitalizations, and lack of adherence to addiction treatment, making the recovery process more difficult.

Co-occurring disorders represent a complex therapeutic challenge that requires a multidisciplinary and coordinated approach. Understanding the reciprocal relationship between mental health disorders and substance use is crucial for developing effective treatment programs that provide comprehensive and focused solutions for this population.

The family of a person struggling with addiction

The family system of an individual on the addiction spectrum may suffer from interpersonal conflicts, significant fluctuations, instability, and mutual dependency between family members, affecting their daily functioning (Tombs, 2005). These challenges are often manifested in mutual anger, feelings of guilt and responsibility among family members regarding the condition of the addicted family member, pain, and even estrangement and distance between family members themselves and from the wider social environment. In many cases, families tend to hide the true situation of the family member from external parties, out of fear of exacerbating their condition or harming their self-image. However, this concealment actually deepens feelings of tension and anxiety among the family. When the father of the family is the one struggling with addiction, distance may develop between him and his spouse, who faces helplessness and frustration while bearing the burden of parenting and financial responsibility alone. Often, a "pathological balance" is created within these families – a situation where the family members of the addicted individual invest significant emotional resources in him, sometimes giving him special attention in the hope of helping him change, but in reality, this complicates his ability to make a real change and optimally deal with the addiction problem (Tombs, 2005). The emotional investment is expressed in various ways, including claims that the family member struggling with addiction is not a sick person, but rather "irresponsible." Sometimes, family members even oppose the rehabilitation processes in which the individual is involved, as they do not believe in his ability to succeed. Moreover, at times the addicted family member serves as a stabilizing factor for the family, as he diverts attention from other everyday problems, such as marital difficulties, financial distress, or domestic violence. In these cases, maintaining the current situation allows the family to delay addressing hidden or overt conflicts and demonstrate flexibility, adaptation, and tolerance toward the addicted family member.

Therapeutic intervention with the family of a person struggling with addiction is essential and can strengthen family interpersonal connections, improve understanding of the patient's struggles, and enhance the individual's motivation to change.

Wives of Men Struggling with Addiction

Codependency is a unique concept that describes behavior patterns in relationships where the man is dealing with addiction. This concept refers to the attempts of his wife to protect him through excessive help, close supervision, and performing actions on his behalf. Although these patterns are intended to assist the man struggling with addiction, they can make the recovery process more difficult (Zaks & Feld, 2005).

Wives of men with addiction problems often experience feelings of lack of identity, guilt, and insecurity. These feelings sometimes lead to people-pleasing behavior toward their partner, even at the expense of their own needs. The wife may subjugate herself to her partner's needs and as a result, feel that she is abnormal compared to her surroundings, retreating into her world and experiencing emotional loneliness and growing distress.

Children in Families with One Parent Struggling with Addiction

Children in families where one parent struggles with addiction are influenced by biological, genetic, and psychological factors, which may lead to feelings of insecurity, confusion, fear, anxiety, and even guilt (Gabriel-Bell & Teichman, 2008). These children tend to develop defense mechanisms, through which they deny the complex situation of their family member and rationalize it to themselves and their surroundings.

Children in these situations may adopt various family roles, including:

- "The Family Hero": A child who tries to do everything "right."
- "The Scapegoat": A child who behaves provocatively or alternatively avoids conflicts.
- "The Adaptive Self": The child creates a barrier between their "true self" and the behavior they show outwardly to fit into the environment and protect themselves emotionally.
- These children often experience constant insecurity, as they see their "true self" as invalid, which manifests in everyday feelings of sadness and shame (Gabriel-Bell & Teichman, 2008).
- Teenagers aged 14–18 living in such families often struggle with forming their personal identity. The anxiety, depression, and sadness they experience due to the father's addiction problems make it difficult for them to resolve conflicts that arose earlier in life, and as a result, they find it hard to develop an individual and mature identity. They remain overshadowed by family conflicts. When one family member is dealing with addiction, the family tends to have "low differentiation," with blurred boundaries and difficulty distinguishing between personal identity and the collective family identity (Gabriel-Fried & Teichman, 2008).

In such cases, there is little patience for the children's needs, and their feelings of loneliness and insecurity are further intensified.

Summary

Populations dealing with addiction, including teenagers, young adults, women, men, and individuals with co-occurring disorders, often face anxiety, shame, insecurity, fear, and a sense of hopelessness for change. Addiction to substances or behaviors negatively impacts the family and close environment, deepening feelings of pessimism and mistrust in the ability to control life and create change. Early and tailored therapeutic intervention can help restore self-confidence, improve adaptability, and enable integration into normative life.

2

TREATMENT FOR ADDICTION

"The most comprehensive formulation of the therapeutic goal and treatment is the striving to live without pretense, to express emotions honestly, and to be true to the emotions and beliefs of the person (the patient) in an authentic way." (Karen Horney)

In addition to enforcement actions, education, and prevention, in recent years, psycho-social and medical treatment has become a significant response to dealing with the use of psychoactive substances and addictive behaviors. Medical treatment primarily focuses on assisting with physical detoxification from substances and providing long-term treatment using substitutes like methadone or Suboxone. Its goal is to ease withdrawal symptoms and stabilize the patient's condition over time. Psycho-social treatment, on the other hand, focuses on understanding the impact of social, environmental, familial, and personal factors on excessive substance use or addictive behavior. It is designed to diagnose the roots of addiction and find effective treatment methods tailored to the patient's individual needs.

Treatment Goals for Addiction:

- Reducing substance use or addictive behaviors or abstaining from them.

- Improving the personal, interpersonal, and social functioning of the patient.

In practice, psycho-social treatment is based on a personal dialogue between the therapist and the patient or within a therapeutic group framework. The treatment focuses on strengthening the motivation for personal change in the realm of substance use, reducing the harm associated with use, cognitive change to adopt adaptive thinking suited to real-life circumstances, emotional change to create positive and strong emotions aligned with life situations, and behavioral change, which includes improving psychological, occupational, and family functioning, as well as developing and strengthening self-control, problem-solving skills, and emotional regulation.

Key Focus Areas of Psycho-Social Treatment:

1. Providing information about the field of addictions and its unique characteristics.
2. Diagnosing and identifying the patient's addiction status and the background to their substance dependence or addictive behavior.
3. Assisting the patient in developing coping strategies and managing a life without substance use.
4. Changing thinking, emotional, and behavioral patterns that maintain the addiction problem (Straussner et al., 2014).
5. Changing personal and interpersonal mental

processes that hinder the reduction or abstinence from substances.

6. Strengthening the language of motivation for change.
7. Empowering the patient and encouraging them to actively confront the problem of substance use (Mignonn, 2014).
8. Identifying Hidden and Visible Strengths of the Patient, Providing Unconditional Support, Problem-Solving, Reducing Hope (De Leon, 2010).
9. Addressing the Patient's Comprehensive Difficulties and Needs.
10. Providing Specific Medical Responses to the Addiction and Related Medical Issues.
11. Vocational Rehabilitation, Advocacy, Acquiring Rights, and Legal Assistance.

PREVENTION AND THE TREATMENT PROCESSES

Prevention of Psychoactive Substance Use

Prevention is a critical first step in addressing the exposure of adolescents, young adults, and adults to psychoactive substances. The approach is multifaceted—spanning educational, social, and treatment-based strategies. Its main goal is to prevent or reduce risky behaviors that could harm the individual or their community. Prevention programs aim to encourage positive health behaviors through social and educational values, reduce the initial use of substances, and prevent continued use by limiting substance availability. They also seek to influence communities and social groups to avoid consumption of harmful substances. For example, prevention efforts in many countries combine strict enforcement against drug trafficking with education and awareness campaigns highlighting the dangers of use (Zimer & Bony-Noh, 2014).

Stages of Preventing Substance Use Among Adolescents and Young Adults

The prevention of substance use is a multi-stage process designed to provide a comprehensive and tailored response to the diverse needs of the target population.

Primary Prevention

Primary prevention focuses on preventing the first-time use of psychoactive substances or the transition from occasional use to problematic, regular use. Strategies include education about addiction and its effects, teaching positive behaviors and values, strengthening personal abilities, and providing alternatives for leisure time (Zimer & Bony-Noh, 2014).

Secondary Prevention

Secondary prevention targets individuals who have already been exposed to substances but have not yet developed problematic patterns of use. The goal is to improve the individual's functioning across social, academic, occupational, and familial domains. This includes counseling, individualized assistance to enhance personal functioning, psychological and functional strengthening, and implementing harm reduction programs.

Tertiary Prevention

Tertiary prevention focuses on populations already dealing with active addiction. This stage includes integrating individuals into psycho-social and medical treatments, helping with rehabilitation, reducing the risk of relapse, and supporting reintegration into the community.

Approaches to Preventing Substance Use

The field of substance use prevention among adolescents, young adults, and adults is based on several theoretical and practical approaches, including the ecological approach and the salute-genic approach. These approaches address systemic, social, and educational aspects of reducing substance use and enhancing the population's ability to cope with risk factors.

The Ecological Approach

The ecological approach views the individual as a holistic system, including the person, their family, their social environment, and the interactions between them. According to this approach, a prevention program should include the following components:

- Raising awareness about the personal, familial, and environmental factors influenced by substance use.
- Strengthening the mental and social resilience of the individual and the community.

- Public education regarding the dangers of substance use, aims to change attitudes that support the legalization of psychoactive substances.

The National Institute on Drug Abuse (NIDA) recommends a comprehensive prevention framework based on evidence-based practices (EBP), which includes working with individuals, families, and communities. These programs involve developing family communication and parenting skills, educating parents and children about substance use, and creating prevention programs from early childhood to high school, with a focus on improving academic achievement, developing social skills, and enhancing personal efficacy. These programs aim to bring about emotional and behavioral change in participants, with an emphasis on tailoring interventions to unique risk factors within the community. However, the ecological approach faces significant challenges, such as increasing public support for the legalization of cannabis and tolerance for the free use of psychoactive substances (Zimmer & Bony-Noh, 2014).

The Salutogenic Approach

The salutogenic approach focuses on identifying factors that promote health among individuals and communities to prevent the use of psychoactive substances (Shagay, 2014). According to this approach, there are pathogenic social factors that contribute to psychoactive substance use, including social legitimization of drug use, free drug trade, and the legalization of psychoactive substances, such as cannabis. In contrast to approaches that focus on pathological risk factors, the salutogenic approach views individuals at the early stages of substance use as a population at risk and in distress, rather than as sick individuals. Therefore, it does not focus on addressing pathological factors, but on the healthy forces existing within the individual and community and strengthening them. An effective prevention program based on the salutogenic approach should include:

- Developing personal skills, strengthening self-confidence, and enhancing personal and community resources.
- Increasing the individual's ability to manage their life and change harmful usage patterns.
- Raising awareness about the dangers of substance use through public campaigns, community prevention workshops, and individual and group therapy for at-risk populations.
- Ongoing evaluation of prevention programs and improving them based on findings.

Research shows that the long-term implementation of the salutogenic approach can change attitudes toward substance use within disadvantaged communities, enhance personal control, and develop a sense of control among participants (Shagay, 2014). Prevention programs based on this approach have been implemented in various countries, including Iceland, the Netherlands, and California, with an emphasis on group workshops for developing social and personal skills, strengthening family bonds, increasing motivation for change, and involving adolescents in proactive activities aimed at enhancing their self-image and sense of control over their lives. Studies have found that participants in these programs reduced or completely stopped substance use, and their sense of efficacy and self-worth increased.

However, despite the prevention efforts made thus far, reports and surveys from recent years indicate a continuous rise in substance use among adolescents, young adults, and adults (WHO, 2018). These data suggest that the existing prevention processes are achieving only modest goals in reducing the phenomenon, while significant challenges continue to face policymakers and professionals in the field. Researchers in the field of prevention emphasize that effective prevention programs must be based on proven scientific knowledge, specifically addressing risk factors and resilience factors, which are key to coping with the issue of psychoactive substance use. Therefore, it is important to give significant weight to these factors when developing new prevention programs to ensure more effective coping with existing challenges.

Outreach and street work

In parallel to prevention efforts in the field of substance use, proactive activity in addressing this issue is carried out through the identification and outreach to individuals using psychoactive substances, either casually or regularly, through street work. The identification and outreach process begins with mapping areas within the community where individuals on the addiction continuum might be found, including streets, malls, parks, clubs, and online spaces. The outreach approach is based on establishing an initial, positive, interpersonal connection between professional counselors or social guides working in the field of addiction treatment and potential clients in places where they are located. The outreach approach focuses on creating a personal connection that strengthens the individual's intrinsic motivation for change. This connection is based on authentic listening to the person's needs and an open, respectful, non-coercive dialogue. Counselors use the "language of change" to empower adolescents, young adults, or adults to engage in addiction treatment and overcome barriers. Ongoing outreach activities, involving a constant presence of professionals and accessibility to them, are a cornerstone for establishing long-term interpersonal connections (Gibson, 2011). As part of the outreach process, there is public education about the characteristics of psychoactive substances, addictive behaviors, and the consequences of use; concrete needs are addressed through instrumental assistance and emergency support, and clients are referred to psychosocial and medical treatment frameworks. An outreach and engagement intervention, which does not focus on direct treatment, can therefore serve as a significant tool for creating contact with populations that avoid seeking help at substance use treatment centers.

However, it should be emphasized that this intervention currently lacks a structured methodology, and systematic evaluation studies have not been conducted to assess its effectiveness in motivating populations along the addiction continuum to engage in treatment. The characteristics of the intervention within the outreach and street work approach vary from place to place. In some cases, the intervention is carried out by guides who lack significant training on the subject, while in other cases, it is implemented by skilled professionals. This situation highlights the need to create a systematic and structured methodology, where the stages of outreach and identification will be defined according to different target populations. Practical tools and processes should be developed to guide the guides and professionals in their work, the roles of the involved professionals should be clearly defined, and evaluation studies should be conducted to examine the effectiveness of the outreach approach. These actions could establish and strengthen informal interventions and transform them into a significant and effective tool for creating interpersonal connections and motivating populations in the process of personal change.

Identification, Diagnosis, and Building an Intervention Plan

The first stage in treating a person dealing with addiction is diagnosis and identification, which occurs through interpersonal acquaintance with the patient. This stage serves as the foundation for building a personalized intervention plan that is tailored to the individual's unique needs and includes emotional and behavioral goals agreed upon between the therapist and the patient. The diagnostic process is based on the therapist's assessment of the factors contributing to the maintenance of addiction, the severity of use, and its consequences on the patient's physiological, mental, and functional state. This assessment includes the following components (Ichot & Smock, 2009):

- Evaluation of the immediate harm experienced by the patient, focusing on identifying dangers and providing solutions such as placing the patient in a safe living environment, reducing and preventing exposure to sexual and physical harm, guiding to a medical framework, and providing instrumental support needed for the continued rehabilitation process.
- Analyzing patterns of psychoactive substance use or addictive behaviors, including the frequency, extent, and compulsiveness of the urge to use substances.
- The history of substance use and its impact on the patient's life.
- Assessment of psychiatric symptoms influencing substance use.
- The patient's general health condition.
- Educational and employment background.
- The existence of a family and social support network.
- Identification of strengths and hidden or visible resources.
- Cultural background, parenting patterns, and general functioning level.

The evaluation process is based on collecting authentic and updated information from various sources, including family members, social, medical, and employment factors, and educational frameworks. In addition, this process places emphasis on identifying everyday problems and the patient's expectations regarding treatment and their future (Ichot & Smock, 2009).

Psychobiological and Psychosocial Tools for Diagnosing Addiction Processes

The diagnostic process in addiction treatment is based on a variety of tools designed to assess the severity of addiction and its effects on the patient's life.

- Self-report by the patient: The patient shares information about their usage patterns, frequency, and the emotional and physiological characteristics associated with it.
- ASI (Addiction Severity Index): A long-standing and central psychosocial questionnaire that evaluates areas such as medical, employment, and legal status, the nature of drug and alcohol use, and the state of family and social relationships (Mclellan et al., 1992).
- Assist: A preliminary screening test designed to identify levels of alcohol and drug use and their impact on the patient's life (WHO, 2010).
- SOGS (South Oaks Gambling Screen): A diagnostic interview tool for assessing the severity of gambling behavior, focusing on the last three months or the past year (Lesieur & Blume, 1987).

- Brain Imaging and Observations: Biological tools that allow monitoring of addiction patterns and their effects on brain activity and physical functioning.

DSM-5: A Key Tool in Addiction Diagnosis

The DSM-5 (Diagnostic and Statistical Manual of Mental Disorders) is an essential diagnostic tool in addiction diagnosis processes. It provides clear criteria for identifying substance addiction and addictive behaviors and serves as a central basis for developing personalized treatment plans. According to the DSM-5, a person is defined as suffering from substance addiction if at least three of the following six criteria are met:

1. Strong cravings or a compulsive urge to use substances.
2. Difficulty controlling the amount of substance used and the time spent using it.
3. Physical withdrawal symptoms when the substance is absent.
4. Development of tolerance, requiring larger amounts of the substance to achieve the same effect.
5. Neglect of activities and interests due to substance use.
6. Continuing substance use despite being aware of the harm it causes (American Psychiatric Association, DSM-5, 2013).

To diagnose gambling disorder, at least four of the following nine criteria must be met:

1. A drive to gamble larger sums to experience a feeling of euphoria.
2. Using gambling as a way to cope with distress, anxiety, or depression.
3. Frequent thoughts about gambling.
4. Difficulty stopping or reducing gambling behavior.
5. Increased restlessness when trying to reduce gambling.
6. Returning to gambling in an attempt to recover financial losses.
7. Loss of social and family connections due to gambling behavior.
8. Taking loans to deal with financial difficulties caused by gambling.
9. Hiding the behavior from close acquaintances.

The diagnostic process in addiction uses a variety of integrated tools, ranging from psychosocial questionnaires to biological tools like brain imaging, as well as the criteria from the DSM-5, which provide a clear and standardized framework for diagnosis. This multidisciplinary approach enables a comprehensive and accurate understanding of addiction and its effects on the patient, improving the alignment of the treatment process with the patient's needs.

Dilemmas in Diagnosis: The Story of Lisa

Lisa, a 26-year-old woman, entered the treatment center hesitantly, as though she wasn't sure she was in the right place. She had been struggling with substance abuse for several years, but her story began long before that; in her first conversation with the therapist, she described a feeling of helplessness that had been with her since she was 18. "I suffer from constant headaches," she said tiredly, "and the anxiety... it's always there, waiting for me."

According to her, she had tried every possible medication – some helped a little, but none of them solved the problem. She even expressed anger towards the medical system that was supposed to help her. "The doctor gave me fentanyl patches a year ago, and it helped a bit, but then... it spiraled out of control. I use large amounts, and when I tried to stop – I just crashed. Depression, extreme fatigue, nothing worked."

Lisa shared that she had recently quit her job as a marketing professional for tech products and that she wasn't sure what the future held for her. She came to the center hoping for answers. "What can you offer me?" she asked almost pleadingly.

"We will start with a structured process," the therapist gently explained. "In the first stage, we will conduct an assessment using questionnaires that will help us understand your addiction, the severity of the issue, and the underlying factors. In the next stage, we will build an intervention plan together, with goals that I believe will help you – such as alleviating the anxiety and reducing your use of medications."

The therapist paused for a moment to ensure that Lisa was following her words. "I can't determine how long the process will take, but this could be an opportunity for you to learn to cope with the situation differently. I recommend starting with physical detoxification from fentanyl and asking your doctor for an alternative medication for your headaches. I'll guide you toward an appropriate medical framework. Later, as part of the treatment, we'll conduct drug monitoring tests to help you maintain 'cleanliness.' What do you think about this approach? Would you be willing to start the treatment process?"

Lisa remained silent for a moment, lost in thought. "Honestly..." she began, searching for the right words, "I'm not sure this is right for me. And this whole drug testing thing—what, you can't trust me?"

The therapist nodded empathetically. "I understand your concern," she said. "The tests aren't meant to doubt you but to help you set boundaries for yourself. It's part of the process we do with most clients here to help them maintain stability. If you relapse, we can recommend further detox and support you along the way. I hope you don't feel this reflects a lack of trust in you."

Lisa sighed. "I'll think about it," she said finally. "I'm just not sure that treatment is what I need right now... I'll let you know."

She stood up and thanked the therapist, but an internal struggle was brewing within her—between her desire to regain control of her life and her fear of what it would demand of her.

The Initial Conversation Between Lisa and the Therapist raises fundamental questions about the diagnostic and intervention methods offered to addiction patients seeking treatment. These questions primarily concern the tension between structured diagnostic processes and the need to build interpersonal relationships and trust between therapists and patients:

- Could the diagnostic and evaluation process undermine patients' willingness to seek treatment?
- Do diagnostic methods hinder the formation of a personal connection between therapist and patient?
- Does the extensive use of psychiatric diagnostic tools (DSM-5, 2013) make it harder for therapists to understand patients' emotional and behavioral characteristics?
- Does focusing on identifying pathological aspects impair patients' ability to recognize their inner strengths and capacity to cope with their difficulties?

In my view, the answers to these questions are affirmative. As Lisa's story illustrates, structured diagnostic processes can sometimes provoke resistance to treatment and impair patients' ability to recognize their inner resources. Studies conducted among addiction therapists confirm that requirements such as drug monitoring tests and participation in long-term diagnostic processes can sometimes hinder the development of a therapeutic relationship and alliance. These actions may convey an impersonal message to the patient rather than fostering a sense of being valued, important, and accepted by the therapist as they are (Shabi, 2023).

Medical Treatment for Addiction

Physical Detoxification from Drugs and Alcohol

The referral process for physical detoxification (detox) from psychoactive substances is carried out by various professionals, including outreach and street workers, family doctors, and therapists in outpatient addiction treatment units. Physical detox is intended for individuals who seek complete abstinence from substance use but are unable to achieve it on their own. Detoxification is conducted in dedicated inpatient facilities operating under the Ministry of Health. This process spans several weeks and includes medical intervention and short-term pharmacological treatment aimed at supporting patients in coping with physical and psychological withdrawal symptoms. These symptoms may include physical pain, gastrointestinal problems, sweating, sleep disturbances, increased heart rate and blood pressure, anxiety, and depression. These symptoms can be severe and intense, sometimes perceived as more difficult than the sensations experienced during substance use itself. Therefore, tailored care is critical to the success of the detoxification process (Wampold, 2009).

Medical Intervention

Medical intervention in the field of addiction, designed for the post-physical detoxification stages, is tailored to the patient's unique needs and focuses on diagnosis, counseling, and medical treatment. This intervention includes an initial evaluation of the patient's substance use patterns, the types of substances previously used, and their physical and psychological effects. Based on this assessment, medical advice is provided regarding recommended treatment strategies. Ongoing medical support involves administering medications, such as methadone and Suboxone, which serve as long-term substitutes for psychoactive substances, helping to prevent relapse (Wampold, 2009). Additionally, medications such as Selincro and naltrexone are used to reduce cravings for psychoactive substances and prevent relapse into addiction. The process includes periodic testing, dosage adjustments, and monitoring of the patient's progress. However, medical and pharmacological treatment alone is insufficient for achieving abstinence or reducing substance use, as addiction is a complex phenomenon requiring a multidisciplinary response (Straussner et al., 2014). Thus, it is crucial to integrate psychosocial therapy into the treatment process. Psychosocial therapy focuses on processing compulsive urges, strengthening self-control, and helping patients modify emotional and cognitive patterns associated with addiction while supporting them in maintaining behavioral change.

In conclusion, medical intervention in addiction treatment is an essential component of the rehabilitation process. However, it must be part of a holistic approach that incorporates emotional, cognitive, and social therapies. Only through a multidisciplinary approach can the complexity of addiction be effectively addressed, enabling long-term change in the patient's life.

Psychosocial Treatment for Addiction

The Motivational Approach: The Language of Change

Following the initial connection with the patient and the physical and pharmacological treatment of their addiction, the next step is to motivate the patient to adopt the "language of change" regarding addiction. This approach, developed by Miller and Rollnick (Miller & Rollnick, 2002), focuses on enhancing the patient's internal motivation and establishing personal and functional change processes through awareness and the use of internal resources.

The stages of change include:

1. Identifying emotions and thoughts related to the change process, even when the problem is not yet fully acknowledged.
2. Processing the patient's ambivalence about change and understanding the conflict between the desire to change and the fear of change.
3. Organizing and making the decision to initiate the change process.
4. Taking active steps to change behavioral patterns and reduce substance use.

5. Maintaining the change, embedding it, and developing an independent and healthy way of life.

Creating stable internal motivation is considered a critical factor in transitioning from one stage to another in the change process (Miller & Rollnick, 2013). Acquiring and internalizing the language of change helps patients undergo personal growth, cope with challenges along the way, and sustain the change over time. However, despite its significant contribution, the motivational approach does not stand alone. It must be integrated with other change-focused approaches, including Cognitive Behavioral Therapy (CBT). CBT can help patients identify and modify the thoughts and emotions that drive addictive patterns while reinforcing adaptive feelings such as self-confidence and self-trust.

In conclusion, the motivational approach provides an effective framework for encouraging patients dealing with addiction to embrace change by empowering their inner strengths and fostering behavioral transformation. Nevertheless, combining this approach with deeper cognitive and emotional processes can significantly contribute to reshaping thought and behavior patterns, helping the patient progress toward a more independent and healthier life.

Cognitive-Behavioral Therapy (CBT) for Addictions

Cognitive-Behavioral Therapy (CBT) is a complementary approach to the motivational framework and is considered one of the leading and most effective methods in psychotherapy for addictions (Marom et al., 2011). This therapy focuses on identifying harmful patterns, altering thoughts and behaviors, and building skills to sustain change over time. It often incorporates additional approaches, such as Contingency Management, to enhance therapeutic effectiveness. The following are the stages of treatment and the key processes involved:

1. Assessment and Identification of the Problem: Understanding the patterns of substance use in the past and present; identifying factors driving the addiction, such as triggers, maladaptive thoughts, and usage prompts; and evaluating the consequences of the addiction on the individual's personal, social, and health aspects.
2. Skill Development and Pattern Modification: Changing thoughts, beliefs, and expectations related to substance use; practicing skills for managing stress and challenging situations; and tailoring the treatment to the patient's individual needs through the development of personalized action plans.
3. Relapse Prevention and Maintenance of Change: Developing strategies for managing risk situations; creating positive experiences that replace substance use, such as rebuilding social and familial relationships; monitoring consumption and documenting progress throughout the process.

The Contingency Management approach, also referred to as a "token economy," is a supplementary tool that promotes positive behaviors through reinforcement. Patients are rewarded for progress, such as abstaining from use, with vouchers or prizes. This approach has proven particularly effective in the initial stages of treatment, although its impact tends to diminish over time if not accompanied by deeper cognitive and emotional changes (Marom et al., 2011).

Cognitive-Behavioral Therapy (CBT) is an effective tool for fostering change among individuals coping with addiction. However, it is not sufficient on its own to achieve long-term reduction or abstinence from substance use. Individuals along the addiction spectrum require a holistic therapeutic approach that addresses multiple aspects of their lives: emotional transformation, fostering personal initiative, problem-solving capabilities, and strengthening and rebuilding supportive relationships. A comprehensive therapeutic response that encompasses all aspects of life enables individuals dealing with addiction not only to adapt to a substance-free reality but also to establish functional continuity and achieve a healthy and meaningful lifestyle.

Treatment for Populations Dealing with Gambling Addiction

Intervention and treatment for populations along the spectrum of gambling addiction, similar to interventions for substance use, begin with motivational engagement to encourage the individual to participate in treatment while simultaneously promoting processes of emotional and behavioral change. These cognitive and emotional interventions aim to reduce harmful behaviors that are maladaptive to their reality, remove barriers to treatment participation, and replace gambling behaviors with positive, adaptive activities. Interventions for individuals facing gambling addiction focus on identifying triggers that contribute to gambling behaviors and practicing alternative responses. Cognitive training for impulse control, altering decision-making patterns, and therapeutic activities that focus on changing attentional biases and maladaptive thinking patterns may empower patients to create meaningful changes (Wiers et al., 2013). Non-invasive brain stimulation targeting the prefrontal cortex has shown promise for helping individuals regulate their neural systems, thereby facilitating changes in gambling-related decision-making patterns. Such stimulation is often conducted alongside psychosocial therapy.

The complexity of treating gambling addiction lies in the difficulty of identifying and reaching this population. Many individuals believe they can stop gambling independently, downplay the personal, familial, and financial harm caused by gambling, and resist receiving treatment alongside those struggling with substance addiction.

Addressing these challenges requires proactive outreach, specialized treatment centers for behavioral addictions, and the integration of psychosocial methods with pharmacological treatments, such as naltrexone or bupropion (Zyban), which have shown effectiveness in treating gambling behavior (Wiers et al., 2013).

Harm Reduction Approach

The Harm Reduction approach focuses on minimizing the potential harms associated with psychoactive substance use rather than strictly aiming to prevent or eliminate use altogether. The goals are to reduce health risks associated with prolonged substance use, improve the individual's daily functioning, and set personalized objectives—whether reducing substance use, continuing controlled use while improving functionality in other areas, or achieving complete abstinence, depending on the individual's choice. This approach incorporates gradual behavioral changes, such as providing guidance toward pharmacological treatments, to support individuals in their unique journey toward healthier lifestyles (Mata, 2021). The uniqueness of the Harm Reduction approach lies in meeting patients "where they are," both in terms of their readiness for change and their personal goals. The therapist assists patients in autonomously choosing their change objectives, even if they continue substance use (Lev-Ran et al., 2014).

However, this approach can leave some patients with feelings of self-disappointment, distress, or insecurity about their ability to reintegrate into society. Therefore, sustained support on the recovery journey is crucial, with an emphasis on strengthening the patient's self-worth to achieve cognitive and behavioral rehabilitation and functional continuity.

Treatment for Populations Facing Addiction

Adolescents

Treatment goals for adolescents on the addiction spectrum focus on providing cognitive and behavioral tools, strengthening problem-solving and self-regulation skills, improving decision-making, teaching relaxation techniques, and fostering assertiveness (Zimmer & Boni-Noah, 2014). A significant emphasis is placed on outreach efforts and street-based work with adolescents, as well as conducting some formal treatment within community settings rather than exclusively in clinical offices. The therapeutic process, often beginning in street-level environments, includes providing initial information on substance use issues, personal counseling, instrumental support, and medical referrals.

In advanced stages, after a meaningful interpersonal relationship is established between the therapist and the adolescent, it is recommended to integrate the adolescent into a specialized addiction treatment framework. Treating this population requires family intervention aimed at promoting family support for the change process and implementing an eco-systemic model that analyzes the connections between the adolescent, school, peer group, legal system, and family. This network analysis, combined with a collaborative action plan involving all relevant parties, strengthens the adolescent's trust in the treatment system, educational framework, and family, encouraging them to adopt the language of change regarding substance use.

Despite these strategies, identifying adolescents using psychoactive substances and integrating them into treatment programs remain challenging. Many adolescents perceive treatment negatively, believing they can manage difficulties on their own, and thus avoid seeking help. Effective treatment for these adolescents requires proactive outreach and consistent, long-term presence in their environments. A high-quality interpersonal relationship between the therapist and the adolescent in the initial stages is key to building trust, forming a therapeutic alliance, and fostering motivation for change. Additionally, from the outset, the treatment focuses on problem-solving and strengthening adolescents' adaptive abilities to support their overall development and recovery journey.

Women

The integration of women into addiction treatment is a complex process influenced by various internal and external factors. On one hand, many women carry a heavy burden of traumas, abuse, rejection, and feelings of humiliation accumulated throughout their lives, especially during their substance use period. Furthermore, many avoid seeking treatment due to shame and fear, particularly fearing the loss of their children if their situation is exposed. These factors create emotional and cognitive barriers that prevent them from reaching out for help. On the other hand, there are also supportive factors, such as family and social support networks, and hidden inner strengths, which can serve as anchors in the change process (Thom, 2010). Moreover, external pressures from the legal system, the community, and the family may encourage women to begin treatment. However, for the treatment to be effective, a unique and sensitive approach is required, one that is tailored to the specific needs of this population. Research emphasizes the need to provide gender-sensitive treatment for women – young women, pregnant women, and mothers – that includes a safe foundation (Secure Attachment) to foster trust between the therapist and the patient, addresses the traumatic experiences and vulnerabilities that shaped their lives, and processes these experiences within a therapeutic framework, with a focus on the connection between substance use and sexual abuse (Gur, 2008). Many women use substances as a way to cope with past traumas or current challenges, and some experience trauma as a result of prolonged substance use. Treatment pathways for these women should include outreach and identification in community settings or digital spaces where they are located, as well as dedicated individual therapy designed to encourage emotional exposure and process traumatic experiences that contributed to their entry into the cycle of addiction or prostitution. The treatment focuses on building a positive interpersonal connection, addressing patterns of pathologization, and processing physical and sexual abuse histories, emotional regulation, and corrective emotional experiences that foster a sense of empowerment and confidence in the process of change regarding substance use. Such tailored treatment may help many women integrate into the process and break free from the cycle of addiction while strengthening their ability to cope with the challenges ahead.

Immigrants

Immigrant communities include individuals who have left their home country and settled in a new country for various reasons: the desire to change their way of life, life-threatening situations in their home country, a wish to improve their economic situation, or the aspiration to live in their homeland. The migration process involves both personal and social challenges, including separation from family and friends in the country of origin, the difficulties of migration itself, and the challenge of adjusting to the new country and integrating into it. Many immigrants try to maintain traditions and customs from their country of origin to preserve a sense of identity and stability. However, the transition to a new country often involves social and familial difficulties, such as unemployment, loneliness, social deviance, connection to marginalized groups, and substance abuse. Treatment for immigrant populations struggling with addiction requires a unique approach to their situation, difficulties, and the cultural gaps they experience during adaptation. Flexible treatment services must be designed to meet the needs of immigrants, recognizing the differences between them and native populations. Services should reflect a culturally adapted perspective and be based on strategies and assessment tools that promote culturally sensitive treatment.

Loue (2002) critiques the one-dimensional view of minority groups affected by addiction, such as immigrants, which are often portrayed solely through a lens of problems or deficiencies. This perspective leads to immigrants not receiving appropriate treatment. The solution to the difficulty in finding suitable treatment staff is to integrate therapists from various disciplines who come from a similar cultural background to that of the patients. These therapists, who speak the patients' native language and understand the cultural context, can strengthen the patients' sense of security and self-esteem. However, it is important to consider the challenges involved in therapy by practitioners from small communities, particularly the concern about breaching patient confidentiality. Immigrant populations dealing with addiction experience significant adjustment challenges in the new country, loneliness, stress, and sometimes self-directed anger over the difficulty of adjusting and stopping substance use. Treating this group requires the use of adapted, research-based treatment models, such as Cognitive-Behavioral Therapy (CBT), which has proven effective in addiction treatment. It is crucial to avoid treating ethnic immigrant groups as a monolithic entity and to ensure accessible treatment that prevents feelings of frustration and insecurity. Targeted treatment approaches enhance the immigrants' sense of optimism and their ability to integrate into the new country while managing their addiction challenges assertively and productively.

Treatment of Trauma and Addiction

Trauma resulting from sexual or physical abuse is a central factor in the development of addiction and mental health disorders among both men and women (Mata, 2021). Treating patients who have experienced trauma alongside addiction requires a focused approach that emphasizes the need to create a sense of safety and protection for the patient. This includes an initial assessment of their current condition and symptoms, without delving too deeply into the traumatic events at this stage. At the same time, the treatment aims to help the patient manage emotional and physiological symptoms originating from the trauma. Trauma treatment for populations dealing with addiction focuses on providing a safe space for the patient to express themselves and share their experiences. This process helps reduce symptoms gradually and fosters effective coping with the challenges of trauma and addiction. Research indicates the effectiveness of integrated treatment that addresses both trauma and addiction simultaneously (Ehlrr & Clark, 2000). This approach has been shown to strengthen the patient relatively quickly and contribute to the development of their sense of capability and self-confidence. One of the proposed models for treating trauma and addiction is Prolonged Exposure (PE) therapy, which is based on confronting the patient with experiences, memories, and thoughts related to the traumatic event. This therapy encourages the patient to face their traumatic memories, process them, and explore the connection between the traumatic memory and substance use. This process allows the patient to develop proactivity and shift maladaptive emotions into strong, constructive ones. Studies indicate that Prolonged Exposure therapy is effective in reducing traumatic symptoms and contributes to a reduction in substance use and medication. However, for some patients, this therapy may be emotionally challenging and intense. In many cases, trauma therapy is conducted prior to addiction treatment. The psychosocial treatment, which may also include medication, aims to strengthen the patients' ability to take control of their lives in the present. It strives to provide them with a sense of self-worth and trust in the therapist, which serves as a foundation for processing the traumatic events they experienced, creating corrective emotional experiences, and motivating them to tackle their substance use problem in the next phase of treatment.

Treatment for Dual Diagnosis

Treatment for populations with dual diagnosis (co-occurring mental health and substance use disorders) focuses on an integrated approach designed to treat both disorders simultaneously (Van Wamel, 2015). This type of treatment requires a clear clinical diagnosis of the mental health condition and a deep understanding of the connection between the mental disorder and addiction, and how they mutually influence each other. The treatment for individuals with dual diagnosis is included in the rehabilitation services for mental health patients and offers a variety of services:

- Psychosocial, and interpersonal support, including guidance, advocacy, and unconditional support.
- Pharmacological intervention is provided under one roof (One-Stop Center).
- Methods such as motivational interviewing and harm reduction programs.
- Vocational rehabilitation (protected employment) that helps build a stable life framework.
- Cognitive-behavioral approaches for preventing substance use relapse.
- Housing programs such as "Housing First".
- Pharmaceutical treatment including Naltrexone, Methadone, and Naloxone.

However, populations with dual diagnosis often "fall through the cracks" in the treatment system. In most psychosocial and medical frameworks, treatment is provided in a fragmented manner that is not coordinated. A comprehensive and integrated approach (One-Stop Center) is needed to provide coordinated and unified treatment. A holistic emotional treatment response – combining cognitive and behavioral approaches, rights exploitation, rehabilitation services, and psychiatric medication management – will help reduce psychiatric hospitalizations, decrease substance use, and ease the patients' rehabilitation process, improving their overall quality of life.

Behavioral Addictions Therapy

Research consistently shows that methods used to treat substance use disorders are also suitable and effective for treating individuals with behavioral addictions, such as gambling, internet addiction, gaming, and sex addiction (Ronzitti et al., 2017). For these populations, the interventions that have proven effective include:

- Cognitive Behavioral Therapy (CBT): Addressing thought and behavior patterns that lead to addiction.
- Motivational Interviewing (MI): Encouraging awareness and behavior change.
- Practice of alternative responses: Changing the response to cues that lead to gambling.

Additional treatments that have been found effective include:

- Psychological therapy focuses on beliefs and thought patterns, Processing false beliefs about gambling behavior, challenging magical thinking patterns, and processing selective memories.
- Transcranial Magnetic Stimulation (TMS): An innovative method using light electrical current to regulate neural activity, which helps reduce impulsive urges and strengthens the ability to delay gratification (Ronzitti et al., 2017).
- Pharmacological treatment: Medications such as

Naltrexone and Nalmefene have been shown to reduce the urge to gamble.

Treating individuals with behavioral addictions presents challenges in identification, as many avoid seeking help due to feelings of shame and a lack of confidence in their ability to change. The treatment system must invest efforts in identifying this population and offer dedicated and tailored treatment for their unique needs, with an emphasis on psychosocial therapy. This type of treatment, based on building an interpersonal relationship between the therapist and the patient and emotional change processes, nurtures belief and self-efficacy regarding changing patterns of addictive behavior.

Family Therapy

Therapeutic intervention with the family of an individual struggling with addiction aims to integrate the family into the rehabilitation process, with a focus on strengthening the patient's ability to reduce or stop substance use (Tombs, 2015). In the early stages of intervention, the goal is to build family narratives based on belief in the patient's ability to make changes, to define boundaries, hierarchy, and roles within the family, and to improve communication among family members.

Intervention with the family of a person dealing with addiction is based on four stages (Tombs, 2015):

1. The "Random" Stage: At this stage, there is

hostility among family members, alongside denial of the severity of the addiction problem.
2. Stage of Open Conflicts: This stage is characterized by accusations being thrown between family members and an attempt to influence the therapist to choose sides.
3. Stage of "Policing": In this stage, family members tend to challenge the boundaries set by the therapist and confront them regarding the intervention process.
4. Stage of Active Participation: In this stage, the family engages in the patient's rehabilitation process, and strengthens and supports them.

Family intervention can have a significant positive impact on the patient's progress. However, due to internal family complexities such as financial conflicts, violence, child-rearing difficulties, and crises between the parents that divert attention from the patient, it often fails to achieve its goals. For the intervention to be effective, it must be time-limited and carried out by a qualified therapist who can steer the conversation in a focused manner. The goal is to engage the family in strengthening the patient while also directing family members to another dedicated therapist for supplementary treatment on pressing family issues.

Group Therapy

Therapeutic groups are a powerful tool for promoting emotional and behavioral change in individuals dealing with addiction. There are various types of therapeutic groups, including task groups, self-help groups such as N.A., and A.A., 12-step programs, educational groups, groups aimed at reducing dropout from therapy, groups for treating violence and substance use, groups to increase motivation for stopping substance use, and groups for preventing relapse.

Led of Therapeutic Groups

Research shows that therapeutic groups lead to significant improvements in patients' conditions. They promote a motivational drive for change, alleviate emotional symptoms, improve the ability to create interpersonal relationships and enhance persistence in abstaining from substances such as drugs and alcohol (Miller & Rollnick, 2013; Yalom & Leszcz, 2019). Group therapy provides a supportive and inclusive framework for populations that often suffer from social isolation. It allows patients to build meaningful interpersonal connections. Receiving support and valuable feedback from Peers, processing harmful behaviors authentically, and drawing inspiration and hope from observing the recovery processes of others – these are components of therapy found to be effective in groups (Yalom & Leszcz, 2019):

- Interpersonal learning: acquiring tools and skills from group interactions.
- Altruism: mutual aid among group members.
- Observing Processes: watching the emotional and behavioral changes of others.
- Catharsis: emotional release and inner cleansing.

- Acquiring Insights: a deeper understanding of personal patterns.
- Modeling: learning by observing individuals who have successfully changed harmful patterns.
- Universality: recognizing that group members share similar experiences and feelings regarding the issue of recovery.

At the core of group intervention lies the corrective emotional experience, which arises from positive interpersonal relationships created within the group. These relationships allow the processing of past experiences and wounds that contributed to the addiction problem. The facilitator of an addiction group is required to guide the group toward mutual listening and reflection of feelings, help in understanding the meaning of group discourse, encourage exploration of "here and now" emotions, present interpretations and insights into required behavioral changes, and foster trust and a sense of belonging among group members. However, the group facilitator could face challenges in leading a group of individuals dealing with addiction, including difficulty in managing conflicts between members, unfocused dialogues that divert attention from the group's goals, lack of trust among certain participants regarding the effectiveness of therapy, and fear of privacy violations that prevent sharing of information. These challenges can be addressed by reflecting group processes back to members, holding open discussions about difficulties preventing progress, engaging in emotional processing that strengthens trust, belonging, and group pride, focusing on problem-solving within the group, and building trust and mutual support.

Self-Help Groups: The 12-Step Program

Self-help groups, such as A.A. and N.A., typically operate without professional involvement. Their main focus is on joint activity and the development of interpersonal connections as a way to cope with addiction. The basic assumption in these groups is that addiction is a disease and that self-control and total abstinence from drugs and alcohol must be promoted. Additionally, there is an emphasis on abandoning the desire to control things outside the individual's control and focusing on a higher power (God) as the source of control, freedom, and happiness rather than relying on oneself (Chen, 2012). The 12-Step Program offers individuals struggling with addiction an opportunity to seek help and accept themselves, become aware of the background that led to their addiction, recognize their personal responsibility for the problem, and take practical steps toward recovery (Ronel, 2020). Studies indicate that group support, acquiring faith in a higher power, and breaking free from social isolation are key factors that help participants in the 12-step program deal with addiction (Chen, 2012). The American Psychological Association (APA, 2017) found that self-help groups reduce the negative effects of prejudice, strengthen feelings of empowerment and personal capability, and provide social support to individuals who have experienced prolonged isolation and insecurity. However, participating in self-help groups alone, without accompanying professional treatment, may make it difficult for participants to deeply understand the sources of their struggles, cope with personal trauma, and make profound emotional and cognitive changes. Combining self-help groups, psychosocial therapy, and pharmacological support may yield the best outcomes: strengthening patients' self-confidence, improving their ability to adapt to life without substance use, and ensuring long-term functional continuity.

Summary: What is Effective Addiction Treatment?

Success in addiction treatment is measured by the reduction or cessation of substance use, as well as by the resolution of related issues and the development of positive attitudes toward substance use. The U.S. National Institute on Drug Abuse (NIDA, 2018) emphasizes that effective treatment requires a combination of medical care and individual and group psychosocial counseling, which should be available and accessible over an extended period. It should address the patient's diverse needs, not just the addiction itself. The Institute also recommends having at least two follow-up meetings with the patient after treatment ends, typically after six months or a year, in order to assess treatment outcomes both in terms of the patient's interaction with the community they live in and how they perceive the changes they've gone through from a long-term perspective.

Evaluating the results of addiction treatment presents challenges (Mignonn, 2014):

- The difficulty in identifying patients who have completed treatment to assess the continuity of results.
- Distinguishing between treatment outcomes for patients without additional problems and those with comorbid conditions (addiction and mental illness).
- Evaluating populations with high mental resilience versus those with low mental resilience.

Therefore, effective addiction treatment should be based on clinical research evidence, provided in an accessible and immediate manner, carried out by a multidisciplinary team, and include early strategies for preventing dropout from treatment. Three months is considered the minimum time required to achieve meaningful change. There are barriers that hinder the achievement of change, some of which are related to the treatment system, and others to the patients themselves. These include financial demands placed on the patient, treatment programs that are not tailored to their needs, fear of social stigma, denial of the addiction problem, the belief that they can recover independently, and a lack of a supportive social and family network.

From the observation of the treatment frameworks presented in this chapter, it appears that treatment outcomes in the field of addiction remain moderate, and there is no psychosocial intervention method that has been definitively proven to be superior to others in preventing dropout and achieving treatment goals. This situation reflects ongoing clinical challenges, including difficulties in diagnosing the unique characteristics of individuals dealing with addiction and understanding them, as well as limitations in implementing treatment methods tailored to patients' personal, cultural, and gender-specific needs. The differences in the application of treatment programs and the absence of personalized models make it harder to achieve treatment goals in the field of addiction and highlight the need for additional therapeutic tools that focus on interpersonal relationships and emotional aspects. Interpersonal therapy and emotion-focused activity – which include processes of emotional awareness, emotional regulation, reflection, and emotional transformation – can serve as valuable tools for strengthening motivation for change, a sense of competence, and control over substance use issues (Shabi, 2024). These approaches, which will be presented in the following chapters, are particularly designed to assist populations experiencing marginalization, difficulty, and distress.

> "A patient will progress toward change if they are attentive and aware of their inner experiences, and if they feel completely free and open to fully expressing these experiences and feelings" (Carl Rogers)

3

INTERPERSONAL THERAPY FOR ADDICTION: STEP BY STEP

"There is no good reason not to grow and change until the last day of our lives" (Karen Horney)

Therapeutic Alliance

Carl Rogers (1957), the father of humanistic psychology, posed several pivotal questions regarding how to help individuals realize their potential and achieve psychological well-being. These questions included: How can we heal populations struggling with difficulty and distress? How can we foster change in people's lives? And what is the significance of the relationship between therapist and client in enhancing the client's capacity for growth and development?

Rogers' conclusion, based on his research, was that a therapeutic relationship characterized by empathy, unconditional support, containment, empowerment, and honesty could serve as the primary foundation for motivating individuals to face their challenges, bring about change, and fulfill their potential (Rogers, 1957). A close, positive, and trustworthy relationship between therapist and client —offering the client a secure base that they may have lacked for many years—is, therefore, the cornerstone of a therapeutic journey aimed at promoting personal change (Rogers, 1962). Throughout this journey, the therapist identifies the client's strengths, resilience, and capabilities, which can replace the feelings of alienation and pessimism that often dominate their life (Yalom, 2002). When it comes to addiction, the therapeutic process focuses on fostering the client's motivation to enact personal change and deepening their awareness of the factors that have thus far hindered them from achieving it (Connors et al., 2013; Prochaska et al., 1992). In a therapeutic journey aimed at recovery from addiction, the client plays an active role in building the treatment framework: defining goals, identifying anticipated challenges—such as difficulties in expressing emotions, emotional regulation, coping with physical and emotional withdrawal symptoms, and managing relapse situations—formulating coping strategies, and strengthening their sense of self-efficacy (Miller & Rollnick, 2013). Designing a mutually agreed-upon framework between the therapist and the client, outlining how emotional and behavioral change will be achieved, constitutes the first and significant step in the therapeutic journey, as illustrated in the therapeutic conversation with Bob.

Bob, a 36-year-old man, sinks heavily into the therapy chair, his eyes shifting uneasily between the therapist's desk and the small window overlooking a gray inner courtyard. This is his first time seeking therapy after years of cocaine addiction.

"The substance helps me cope," he begins in a quiet, almost apologetic tone. *"I've been carrying this gloom for years, and sometimes... it's like it gives me a push. I feel more energized, alive for a moment."*

Bob lives alone in a small apartment and maintains

minimal, if any, social connections. According to him, he doesn't truly believe that anything can help him. *"My mom pushed me to come,"* he says. *"She kept nagging me until I agreed."*

The therapist seeks to explain the meaning of therapy to Bob. *"I see it as a sort of shared journey,"* she says. *"The goal isn't just to confront the difficulties but also to heal, to discover new things about yourself.* I believe that the relationship between us can help you better cope with the sadness and melancholy that accompany you. "Bob lifts his gaze, skepticism evident in his expression. "Do you really think that's possible?" he asks.

"Your ambivalence about this process is understandable," she responds. "I believe in your ability to change, and I'll be here for you every step of the way, listening and supporting you. But I also need your presence, your willingness to try."

Bob lowers his eyes. "I don't know," he says. "I don't believe in myself... These goals seem impossible to me. I'll have to think about it."

Two days later, the therapist's office phone rang. "It's Bob," he said over the line. "I thought about what you said. Maybe... maybe something good could happen after all."

The therapeutic journey aimed at changing patterns of addiction presents unique challenges for therapists, especially when working with clients who lost trust in people and in the concept of therapy itself. Prolonged experiences of rejection and a lack of support over the years deepen their skepticism about the effectiveness of therapy in creating change (Timulak, 2017). Another challenge lies in the difficulty clients face in establishing a secure foundation with the therapist. They often wonder if the therapist will stand by them, be attentive to their needs, and maintain a consistent presence. These concerns stem from traumatic experiences of emotional loneliness, deprivation, and harm in interpersonal relationships, both past and present (Shaver et al., 2005). To address these challenges, therapists should explore the client's previous attempts at therapy early in the relationship to understand why they failed to achieve their desired goals. It is also crucial to introduce the client to the emotionally focused interpersonal framework that will guide the therapeutic process and clarify the importance of emotional change in enabling behavioral change (Greenberg, 2017). The core message the therapist must convey to the client is one of unconditional acceptance, delivered with a positive attitude and genuine care (Connors, 2013; Furrow et al., 2022). Ensuring a secure base and reinforcing the client's trust in the therapist and the process are fundamental principles of an effective therapeutic journey. At the same time, it is essential to address emotions tied to self-doubt, anger, and anxiety, particularly in light of the uncertainty inherent in the process. Through reflection and emotional mirroring, clients can gain insight into the emotional patterns they experience in the present—such as feelings of loneliness and hopelessness—and develop a willingness to confront the emotional difficulties that will arise along the journey, including the challenges of substance withdrawal.

Another foundational principle is tailoring the paths to change to the client's specific needs, recognizing that the therapeutic journey is not linear. It may include twists, obstacles, moments of progress, and even a sense of stagnation (Prochaska et al., 1992). The shared process and mutual commitment between therapist and client are the keys to fostering genuine change (Shaver et al., 2005), as illustrated by David's story.

David, who has struggled with heroin addiction for many years, begins therapy after dropping out of four previous treatment programs. "I just don't have the patience for the whole idea of therapy," he says candidly during his first session with the therapist.

His mistrust is evident, but the therapist focuses on creating an open and honest connection. "I understand that it's hard for you to trust, and therapy is indeed complex and not always straightforward," she says. "But I'm not here to impose anything on you. I'm here to work with you. Together, we'll try to figure out what's holding you back, what's making it hard to take the first step."

David lifts his gaze for a moment, reflecting. "Look," he says, "after everything I've tried, I just don't believe therapy can help me. I'm mostly here because of court pressure. I don't want to go back to prison. But honestly? I'm a closed-off person. I struggle with relationships—with myself, with other clients I don't trust, and with therapists. It all takes effort I just don't have the energy to put in."

The therapist remains silent for a few moments before saying, "I hear you, but I also hear something else between your words. You're saying you came here because of the court, but I wonder if there's a small part of you, even the tiniest bit, that thinks maybe—just maybe—change is possible."

David lets out a bitter laugh. "Me? Change? Look at my life," he says, shaking his head.

"I know your situation is tough, and I know you've faced failures in the past," the therapist responds gently. "But I see something different in you. Maybe it's the voice that brought you to this session despite everything. Let's start with one small step—just one. We don't need to think about the whole journey right now. I'm here, and we can take this on together, at your pace. I'm very optimistic about you."

David examines the therapist's face, trying to gauge the sincerity in her words. Finally, he leans back with folded arms and says quietly, "Maybe. I'm not promising anything, but maybe I'm willing to try."

"That's enough for me," the therapist says with a smile. "One small step. Together."

Building a therapeutic alliance, as David's therapist attempted to do, serves as a central source of strength in driving an interpersonal therapeutic journey. David's engagement in the process was grounded in the therapist's clear messages: unwavering commitment to the journey, unconditional support, and genuine optimism about his ability to succeed, achieve emotional change, and recover from addiction. One critical step in advancing the therapeutic process, particularly in the field of addiction, involves exploring the client's ambivalence about change.

This requires a thorough evaluation and reflection on the arguments for and against change. At the outset of the journey, it is not necessary to overwhelm the client with extensive concrete goals. Instead, the focus should be on general objectives that reinforce the client's self-worth and confidence (Naar & Safren, 2017; Magill et al., 2018). At the same time, it is essential to foster positive expectations and instill hope, laying the foundation for eventual change (Greenberg et al., 1996; Degnan et al., 2014). The therapeutic journey is grounded in principles of unconditional support, empathetic listening, and containment (Yalom, 2002; Bowlby, 1988). These principles are especially significant for clients in severe distress, such as those suffering from addiction, as they provide a sense of trust in their ability to face challenges. The support offered by the therapist, in conjunction with emotional and behavioral change processes, enables the client to envision the goal on the horizon—health and independence. The way clients evaluate their therapeutic journey, aimed at achieving change and recovery from addiction, depends on the depth of their experience: the extent to which trust and hope were instilled in them, the bond formed with the therapist, and the feeling that they are not alone. This can be seen in the story of Sarah.

Sarah sits in the closing session with her therapist, her eyes sparkling. "This journey will never truly end for me," she says. "I know it's a constant personal struggle to preserve everything I've worked so hard to achieve." According to her, after years of addiction to prescription drugs, the therapeutic process gave her not only tools for coping but also a sense of confidence and self-belief. She emphasizes that her ability to endure the therapeutic journey was directly tied to the interpersonal bond that developed between her and her therapist. "You were my anchor, my support," she adds.

From the very first day, the therapist shared every single detail of the therapeutic framework with Sarah. There was no sense of concealment or distance—everything was open and clear. "You supported me, understood me, and cared for me without limits," Sarah describes with gratitude.

Despite the ups and downs throughout the difficult struggle to stop using medication, there was one thing Sarah always knew for certain: she was not alone. "There was someone who accepted me as I am, someone who stayed with me every step of the way. I wasn't alone in this journey, and that's what gave me the strength to keep going."

In conclusion, an authentic relationship between therapist and client, one that integrates empathy, acceptance, support, and honesty, is a cornerstone of the therapeutic journey. When the therapist outlines the characteristics of the journey and its complexities while emphasizing the client's freedom to choose whether to participate in the process of emotional and behavioral change, they strengthen the client's sense of optimism and belief in their ability to succeed and achieve healing and transformation (Degnan et al., 2014). An individual's ability to successfully complete the therapeutic journey while facing addiction depends largely on their capacity to overcome the personal and social barriers in their path. Sensitive and well-informed treatment enables the client to carefully remove those barriers and move forward toward self-realization and recovery—more on this in the next section.

> "The ability to achieve a good life is not a static state but a shared journey between therapist and client, a process of choosing among possibilities and striving forward—the therapeutic journey is the direction, not the destination" (Carl Rogers)

A Roadmap Centered on Emotions

> "What is required to enable change and growth in a client is a shift in their self-awareness" (Maslow)

"I don't know how it happened again," Paul says in frustration. "I'm just drawn to it as if I have no control." For the past five years, Paul has been struggling with his addiction to online gambling. Over the last two years, his situation has worsened, and he has lost staggering amounts of money. "It's not just the money," he adds. "It's the anger at myself, at the fact that I don't learn my lesson. I just can't understand why I can't control it. There's some kind of barrier in me that I can't figure out."

The therapist listens to Paul with empathy, and Paul concludes in a whisper, "I'm hopeless. I don't see how anything can change. I have no future."

In his book *On Becoming a Person,* Rogers describes the importance of extending a helping hand to individuals facing personal, emotional, familial, and social barriers—such as those described by Paul —which often stem from feelings of anxiety, depression, shame, and sadness following traumatic experiences like abuse, rejection, neglect, and humiliation (Rogers, 1951). These barriers hinder clients from achieving full functioning, realizing their potential, and attaining a fulfilling life (Rogers, 1961). To help clients overcome these obstacles, Rogers presents a kind of "roadmap" for therapy. This roadmap is based on emotionally focused interpersonal actions aimed at deepening the client's awareness of the roots of their struggles. It includes careful attention to their needs, acceptance of their emotions and complex experiences, and an uncompromising attitude of empathy, warmth, care, and acceptance (Rogers, 1951). Rogers emphasizes that emotional and functional change arises from therapeutic relationships characterized by genuineness, the therapist's consistent presence in the client's life, the strengthening of the client's self-worth, and a deep understanding of their needs (Rogers, 1961). This approach is practically demonstrated in a therapeutic conversation with Robert.

This is not Robert's first time seeking therapy, but it is the first time he has come voluntarily, without external pressures. Robert, 35 years old, has been using cocaine intermittently for the past twelve years. In the past, his family forced him to participate in a physical detox program and later in psychosocial therapy, but he could not persist in either.

Now, as he sits across from the therapist, exhaustion is evident in his expression. "I want to give myself a chance to change," he says. "I've had a few panic attacks over the last two years, and they really scared me. I tried medication, but it didn't help much. A few months ago, I decided to stop using cocaine because I thought it was causing my anxiety. Instead, I started using cannabis, but that's not helping either. I feel depressed… I just don't know what to do."

The therapist allows him to express his feelings without interruption. When he finishes, she gently says, "I hear your sadness and the helplessness you're experiencing, but I also see that you're here, talking, sharing, and trying to understand what's happening to you. You have a genuine desire and inner strength to deal with what's holding you back, don't you?"

"Yes, maybe," Robert responds thoughtfully. "I'm really trying, but… I keep wondering if it's hopeless. I have so many problems, I don't even know where to start. And these panic attacks…" He pauses for a moment and takes a deep breath. "They're the worst feeling in the world."

The therapist nods. "I understand how hard it is to struggle with addiction for so many years," she says empathetically. "I'd like us to work together to understand what's blocking you from stopping the substance use and what's causing the anxiety you're experiencing. I know you're in deep distress right now, but I'm here to walk this journey with you, hand in hand. You have the willpower, Robert, and I believe in your ability to change. I'm optimistic. With the right support, I truly think you can feel better."

Robert's expression softens. While he isn't entirely sure what he believes at this moment, something in her words touches him, perhaps even igniting a small spark of hope.

The therapist's actions, aimed at helping Robert remove obstacles and ease his therapeutic journey, reflect the humanistic approach. This approach, centered on empathetic listening unconditional support and honestly, may represent a significant step both in deepening Robert's awareness of the roots of his struggles and in developing his self-efficacy to initiate change. Nevertheless, the humanistic approach has faced criticism over the years. Critics have questioned whether its central tools—empathy, unconditional support, and genuineness—are sufficient for processing intrapersonal conflicts and achieving meaningful change, particularly among populations experiencing severe distress (Wachtel, 1993; Timulak & Mcelvaney, 2018). Various studies have addressed this critique by emphasizing the need to expand the humanistic approach through deeper, dynamic psychological exploration. This exploration focuses on processing early contributing factors to anxiety and trauma—common characteristics among individuals along the addiction spectrum (Wachtel, 1993). Other studies have highlighted the effectiveness of methods developed from the humanistic approach, such as Emotion-Focused Therapy (EFT), in addressing intrapersonal conflicts, anxiety, and trauma (Johnson, 2019; Greenman & Johnson, 2013). Techniques like emotional inquiry, reflection, emotional mirroring, and strengthening the client's ability to express emotions to the therapist help the client understand the roots of their feelings, identify contributing factors to their trauma, and encourage a process of transformation (Johnson, 2019; Greenman & Johnson, 2013). In the advanced stages of Emotion-Focused Therapy, it is possible to achieve significant transformation in emotions like anxiety and depression, converting them into feelings of security and control. This change can provide clients with a sense of resilience and capability, enabling them to overcome behavioral barriers and ultimately leading to meaningful pattern changes in their addiction.

In conclusion, the removal of barriers to recovery from addiction and the achievement of personal transformation, as proposed by humanistic psychology and Emotion-Focused Therapy, is based on close relationships between the therapist and the client. These relationships are characterized by the therapist's uncompromising empathy, unconditional support for the client's strengths and abilities to change, and consistent, meaningful presence in the client's life (Shabi, 2022; Greenberg, 2015). The therapist and the quality of the connection they establish with the client play a unique and significant role in driving the process of change. This connection enables the client to gain deep insights into maladaptive emotions, such as anger and insecurity, and to learn how to regulate them. Over time, this process can lead to the transformation of these emotions into empowering feelings of capability and strength (Greenberg, 2017). These changes contribute to effectively addressing fundamental barriers in the client's life, both personally and functionally. Among other things, they assist in reducing or ceasing substance use and promoting social adaptation (Shabi, 2024). On the topic of unconditional support, which is one of the most central and impactful tools in removing personal barriers among individuals struggling with addiction, we will delve further in the next section.

Unconditional Support

Jeff, a 33-year-old single man, enters the therapy room with a pronounced limp, his expression revealing sadness and exhaustion. "I don't know how anything can change," he says. "I'm only here because they told me you might be able to help me find a job." Jeff has been struggling with an addiction to amphetamines for nine years. "I need it like air to breathe," he sighs, "it's the only thing that makes me feel... like I'm alive." A severe injury has left Jeff disabled, dependent on a disability allowance from the National Insurance Institute. His relationship with his family is fragile, and he finds it hard to believe he can make any changes in his life. Jeff has sought therapy for help in integrating into supported employment.

How can we assist people like Jeff, who live in a closed world, experience sadness and despair, and do not believe in themselves? Rogers viewed the process of unconditional acceptance and support as a fundamental principle that enables a person to feel loved, important and wanted. It helps alleviate the experience of loneliness and despair that accompanies their life and fosters a meaningful connection between them and the therapist (Rogers, 1951). Based on this perspective, the person-centered approach was developed, emphasizing the importance of acceptance, support, and containment, especially for populations facing severe distress (Greenberg, 2010).

The language of unconditional support is based on positive and supportive regard for the efforts the patient makes over time to change (Prochaska et al., 1992). Person-centered interpersonal dialogue aims to provide a safe foundation, allowing patients to express their feelings openly, with the understanding that their emotional needs —such as feelings of shame and despair—are acknowledged and accepted. These actions help patients to let go of feelings of guilt and discomfort about themselves, both in the immediate and long term (Rogers, 1957, 1995). The power of unconditional support can restore a sense of self-worth and trust in oneself after years of deprivation of such support (Oxley, 2011). In the language of acceptance and positive support, attentive feedback and reflection of the patient's words take place (Greenberg, 2004). Listening and reflecting sometimes involve repeating the patient's words verbatim, with the aim of highlighting their strengths and enhancing their awareness of their personal abilities. A more complex reflection, such as "predicting the next move," allows the therapist to process and interpret words and sentences the patient did not explicitly say, with an emphasis on identifying potential for change, assertiveness, and independence (Connors, 2013). Optimal reflection depends on how well the patient understands and connects with the therapist's messages and how much they express emotions, reflect on them, and examine their sources (Johnson & Campbell, 2022). Positive support is also crucial in the face of challenges such as substance use relapse and functional, occupational, or social difficulties. A therapist who reinforces the patient's honesty, efforts to reduce substance use, and persistence in therapy encourages the patient to believe in their ability to change and adapt to a normative life (Shabi, 2024). Furthermore, support for the patient must be an ongoing process—at each therapy session, it is essential to repeatedly express genuine appreciation for their attempts to change (Yalom, 2019). The conversation between Sandra and her therapist exemplifies the language of unconditional support.

Sandra enters the therapy room and sits down heavily in front of the therapist. "I feel depressed," she says. "All my attempts to stop gambling have failed. I try everything – not carrying my phone, disconnecting from the computer, even avoiding lottery stations. Nothing works. I keep going back to it, again and again, like it's a possession. I'm really suffering."

"I hear your pain," the therapist responds gently. "You're putting in so much effort to stop, but you feel stuck. You're facing this alone, without support from your family, and with financial debts weighing on you. This is a great pain, and I'm here to listen."

Sandra nods, tears welling up in her eyes. "Exactly," she whispers. "I'm in complete depression, confused, with no direction. There were times when I stopped gambling and worked as a secretary. It seemed like everything was falling into place, but it was only for a short time. All the money I earned went back into gambling, and my relationship with the kids has completely broken down. I think... something inside me is just not right."

The therapist looks at Sandra with empathy and encouragement. "I really appreciate your honesty and sharing," she says. "It's not easy to admit all of this, but the fact that you're here shows immense strength. I also hear that in certain periods, you managed to change your life, make good decisions for yourself, and show capability and potential. There's no reason why that can't happen again."

Sandra hesitantly raises her gaze. The therapist's words slowly penetrate the veil of despair that surrounds her.

"I'm here with you," the therapist continues. "Together, we'll try to understand the factors behind the addiction and what makes it hard for you. We'll consider how to break the ice with your children and rebuild your relationship with them. The children can be a significant and meaningful factor in your path to change. I believe in you and your strength, Sandra. You are not alone on this journey."

The integration of unconditional support for Sandra, as well as for other patients, is primarily aimed at instilling optimism in her ability to create change. Patients begin to experience a sense of capability and self-trust when they recognize the strengths and abilities within them that they can use to face the challenges ahead (Shabi, 2024). Accepting a person as they are, with containment and encouragement, can create a corrective therapeutic experience even for patients who are disillusioned and in severe distress (Furrow et al., 2022). When the therapist expresses positive emotions toward the patient's personal story and how they have dealt with challenges in the past, this reveals the inner strengths and abilities they possess to adapt to complex realities, thus strengthening their sense of self-worth (Goldman & Greenberg, 2015). In the spirit of unconditional support, when patients express resistance or show indifference to the language of support, the therapist should avoid confrontation and criticism (Miller & Rollnick, 2013). Instead, they should focus on understanding the feelings underlying the resistance, process the hidden emotions, which may include anger and despair, and work with the patient to find ways to change these patterns. This approach conveys to the patient that the support they receive is not contingent on their behavior or actions and that their life's complexity and experiences are acknowledged (Shabi, 2024). In other words, the language of unconditional support includes encouragement, reinforcement, acceptance, care, and concern without conditions. It is free from judgments and barriers and aims to create a safe and empowering experience for the patient (Rogers, 1951).

Unconditional Support Language: Therapist to Patient Feedback

- "I have complete trust in you and your ability to change."
- "I am with you every step of the way."
- "I sense that you have strengths you haven't yet identified, which can help you heal."

- "I appreciate the great efforts you're making to cope and not give up."
- "You have the ability to move forward and persist, even when the path seems difficult."
- "I'm here for you! Together, we'll try to face the challenges on the road to recovery."

In conclusion, unconditional support language should be employed throughout all stages of person-centered emotional therapy. It includes expressing positive emotions, encouragement, and reinforcing the patient while highlighting their hidden and apparent strengths. Its purpose is to give the patient a sense of being important, wanted, loved, and accepted, and to motivate them to believe in their ability to take control of their life and face personal difficulties, including addiction, in a proactive manner. Studies show that unconditional support language strengthens marginalized populations, encourages emotional reflection, and improves self-worth, capability, and trust in the ability to change (Greenman & Johnson, 2022; Greenberg, 2004).

An empathetic understanding of the internal experiences of a person dealing with addiction is a complementary element to unconditional support language – and this will be discussed in the next section.

> "When the patient is hurt, anxious, and doubts their self-worth, genuine understanding, and listening are needed to eventually allow for change." (Carl Rogers)

Empathy

> "We think we listen, but we seldom listen with real understanding and true empathy. Empathetic listening is one of the strongest forces for change that I know." (Carl Rogers)

Jason sits on the therapy couch with his head lowered and his hands clasped, looking restless. Alcohol has been a constant companion in his life for sixteen years. "When I drink," he tells the therapist, "it feels like everything stops. I get some peace, and that's all I need sometimes."

He lives alone in a small apartment, surviving on a disability allowance granted to him due to his addiction problem. His life has become very limited – no job, no social connections, and no hope for a better future.

"I don't see how anything can change," he adds. "It won't get better. Nothing will change for the good."

How can we help patients with passive behaviors, like Jason? Are the interpersonal processes offered by humanistic psychology capable of instilling optimism and hope in populations that experience social isolation, anxiety, and low self-esteem?

According to Rogers, this is possible through close interpersonal relationships, unconditional acceptance, and empathetic understanding of the human mind and its world (Rogers, 1962). Rogers referred to the language of empathy as an attempt to accurately understand the patient's feelings here and now, connecting to vulnerable emotions such as anxiety and shame, and encouraging the patient to express their feelings and understand their origins (Jacobs, 2013; Rogers, 1951). Kohut also views empathy as an active tool for psychological and emotional understanding of the person. According to him, the therapist is not just a listener but also thinks, feels, and experiences the patient's inner world (Kohut, 1982). This therapeutic action involves trying to identify the patient's emotional state, experiencing emotions similar to those they are feeling, and deeply understanding their sensations. Many studies show that empathy is a critical tool for creating an authentic and deep connection with the patient, and it strengthens their ability to take the first step toward emotional change (Maibom, 2012; Greenberg, 2015; Miller & Rollnick, 2013). Empathy is not just a psychological mechanism of identification; it is also an active process that enables interpersonal connection and changes in emotions such as anxiety and sadness (Maibom, 2012). In order for a patient to experience empathy, they need an external figure to identify with their feelings, and therefore, empathy can only exist in genuine human interactions (Agosta, 2018).

The language of empathy, especially with individuals dealing with addiction, requires deep listening, full attention, and a sincere effort to truly understand their inner experiences. Rogers emphasized that empathy means the therapist's ability "to put themselves in the patient's shoes as if it were themselves" (Rogers, 1957). Authentic connection with the patient only occurs when the therapist succeeds in fully listening to them and identifying their difficult and maladaptive emotions. Such a connection deepens the patient's awareness of their emotions, strengthens their ability to express them, and enables them to create change in their beliefs about them (Greenberg, 2010). The therapeutic conversation with Deniel illustrates how the language of empathy works.

When Deniel, a thirty-five-year-old man, enters the therapy room, it is clear that he carries a heavy load of experiences and disappointments. Deniel has been using cannabis intensively since he was seventeen. "It's my solution," he tells the therapist. "It's the only thing that calms me from these feelings – confusion, anger... things I don't really understand. I think it's connected to all the violence I experienced at home when I was a child."
Deniel shares with the therapist that he had previously tried to integrate into two therapeutic frameworks but did not manage to stay in either.
The therapist carefully chooses her words. "I hear your sadness," she says. "What you've experienced in your family – the violence, the loneliness. I also sense your current attempts to understand why you feel stuck when it comes to stopping cannabis use. You show a deep awareness of what you've experienced and the connection between these experiences and your use of the substance."
"In the materials. I appreciate your honesty and your efforts to share. This is the beginning of the road to change."
Deniel nods slowly, thoughtfully. "Yes, I talk about it," he says, "but the truth is, I don't know what to do. I'm not

sure I have the strength to start therapy again. I really want to stop, but... I'm just not sure I'll succeed."

"I feel your difficulty," the therapist says warmly, "Starting therapy again, facing the pain and the difficult memories once more – it's not easy. You have a lot to deal with: sadness, insecurity, those feelings you've been carrying for years. I also sense your distress over the disconnection from your family, the fear of experiencing pain again in therapy, as you did before, and the fear that all your efforts won't lead to the peace you're looking for. Is that right?"

Deniel straightens a bit in his chair, a spark of hope lighting up in his eyes. "Yes," he whispers, "that's exactly it. I just don't know how to begin."

The therapist's attempts to put herself in Denial's shoes, to feel as closely as possible the pain and sorrow he's experiencing, and to convey that to him, are described as an act of "empathetic motivation." This action aims to strengthen Denial's self-awareness, with the goal of giving him a sense of security in dealing with his emotions, encouraging emotional change, and reducing feelings of loneliness and insecurity that have accompanied him for years. The language of empathy, grounded in the therapist's deep emotional identification with the client, is a central pillar of the emotion-focused interpersonal therapy process (Greenberg, 2017). It is based on an authentic understanding of the client's experiences and a deep knowledge of the emotional barriers formed due to past trauma. Its purpose is to respond to the deep need of vulnerable populations to feel understood and valued

(Agosta, 2015). This process simplifies therapy and enables clients to abandon problematic patterns that have developed in their relationships. While empathy alone is not enough, in order to bring about significant emotional and behavioral changes, the client's internal psychological conflicts must be processed (Wachtel, 1993). However, empathy allows the therapist to create a new narrative for the client's emotional experience and to support them in releasing difficult emotions and processing conflicts, similar to dynamic therapeutic processes (Oxley, 2011). The therapist must constantly ask themselves whether they are connecting to the client's vulnerable emotions and if the empathy they are using resonates with the client. An empathetic failure may occur when there are gaps between the therapist and client regarding the therapeutic framework or treatment goals when there are differences in their worldviews, or when the therapist struggles to understand the client's words. A situation where the client feels misunderstood or lacks genuine listening may disrupt the therapeutic process (Agosta, 2018). To address empathetic failures, the therapist must consistently check with the client if the emotional process is understood. The therapist must ensure that the interpretation they give of the client's emotions and experiences is clear, grounded, and aligned with the reality of the client's life (Agosta, 2010). Such an interpretation, provided within the framework of active empathy language, can lead the client to a more proportional reflection of their emotional experiences, the release of maladaptive emotions, and their transformation into more adaptive and effective feelings (Agosta, 2018).

Empathy language: Therapist feedback to the client

- "I feel that the barriers you experience in your relationship with your family are the foundation for the sadness and despair that you are feeling during this time."
- "I sense that you are feeling guilty today because you couldn't control yourself and express your feelings during your meeting with your therapy group members."
- "Is the return to drug use merely a way to cope with the anxiety and pain you feel due to the disconnection from your children?"
- "I sense that the message you've received over the years, that you're a failure, still resonates with you and contributes to your current insecurity. How do you experience what I'm pointing out? Am I reading you correctly?"
- "Do you sometimes feel disappointment and frustration with how the therapy session is unfolding right now?"

A therapeutic conversation with Kevin demonstrates how empathy language operates while checking whether the interpretative processes for his emotional background are penetrating his heart and are understandable to him.

Kevin, a forty-three-year-old man, has been using cannabis and alcohol for sixteen years, but the past year has been the hardest for him. "I left home," he tells the therapist in a grim tone, "I separated from my wife. I cut ties with the kids. It's all because I just can't stop using." The pain in his words is evident, and he looks sad and restrained. "I'm hopeless about myself," he adds, "Every time I tried to stop, I failed."

Throughout the conversation, the therapist attempts to engage him, but every time she touches on his emotions, Kevin goes silent. After one of these silences, she gently addresses him, " Kevin, I notice that we've had many silences today. I want to understand how you're feeling in our conversation. I also sense that your disconnection from your family and children, along with the return to heavy cannabis use, are contributing to your frustration and lack of trust in yourself. Is something in the questions I've asked difficult for you?"

Kevin takes a deep breath. "The truth is," he says candidly, "it's not the questions. It's just... I don't see a way forward. I'm not sure these sessions will help me see my kids or change anything. I really don't know what will happen."

The therapist looks at him encouragingly and says, "I hear you, Kevin, and I want to address what you've raised. But before we do that, let's look at what's happening between us right now. I sense that you're distant from me today, and that's very different from our previous sessions. I wonder if the physical disconnection from your family and children is making you think that our connection here might also end and that in the end, you'll be left alone again, feeling helpless. Am I understanding you correctly?"

Kevin looks at the therapist for the first time. "Maybe," he whispers.

In summary, the use of active-interpretive empathy language for individuals dealing with addiction is a vital component throughout the emotional-focused interpersonal therapy process. Its purpose is to provide clients with recognition and support, deepening their awareness of their emotions, while avoiding judgment or negative evaluation (Agosta, 2010, 2015). This language, based on a deep emotional connection between the therapist and the client, goes beyond simple identification processes; it involves actively deepening the client's awareness of the background behind their maladaptive emotions and providing interpretations that help uncover their sources. The therapist motivates the client to express emotions freely and constructively while developing insights into inhibiting emotional patterns. This process serves as a pathway for emotional transformation – a central goal in emotion-focused therapy – and aims to help clients develop strong feelings of self-control and capability (Greenberg, 2015). These emotions eventually manifest in behavioral changes, problem-solving, and a reduction or cessation of substance use. Empathy language is based on creating honest and respectful relationships between the therapist and the client. These relationships are characterized by a blend of empathy and identification with the difficulty of change and support for the client's efforts to make changes. The language of honesty, which complements empathy language in emotion-focused interpersonal therapy, is discussed in the following section.

> "The meaning of being empathetic is a deep understanding of the client. Understanding their inner feelings accurately, understanding the emotional components of their experiences and their significance, as if the therapist were experiencing those feelings themselves" (Carl Rogers)

Honesty

Carol, a twenty-nine-year-old woman, enters the addiction treatment center with some hesitation. Since her military service, cannabis has been a part of her life, but she doesn't see it as a problem, but rather as a habit. "I don't really understand why my doctor decided to send me for treatment," she tells the therapist, "Yes, I use cannabis, but I'm not addicted. I can handle my problems on my own."

The therapist listens to her words and tries to understand what those difficulties are, but Carol immediately shuts down and refuses to elaborate. The conversation becomes a cycle of denial and withdrawal.

At the end of the conversation, the therapist reviews the psycho-social and medical information at her disposal and discovers that the situation is more complicated than Carol is willing to admit. She may be dealing with deeper distress, for which cannabis serves as an emotional "Band-Aid." The therapist wonders how she can reach Carol, encourage her to speak honestly about her situation, and possibly touch on a place that might make her start considering change.

In emotion-focused interpersonal therapy, the language of honesty between the therapist and the client is expressed on two levels: the first level is that of the therapist, who offers the client genuine, real, and authentic attention. This is done through expressions of support, empathy, and giving open feedback about the client's honesty, efforts, strengths, and ability to cope and create change. The therapist's honesty language focuses on interpersonal dialogue that encourages the client to deepen their awareness of their emotional experiences and behaviors and understand their background (Shabi, 2024). The therapist observes the client's internal experiences and reflects them for the client, thus strengthening the client's willingness to examine the background of their emotional and behavioral patterns and consider positive alternatives (Meier et al., 2005).

The second level is that of the client, which relates to the honesty they demonstrate in the therapeutic process. This involves their ability to freely and authentically express their emotions, present their current situation, and examine their personal patterns. When the therapist acts with transparency and integrity, without pretense or manipulation, they help the client stay connected to themselves and express their emotional experiences freely (Tudor & Merry, 2006). In Carol's case, the therapist can encourage her to be honest about her difficulties and situation if she operates with transparency and full sharing of the information at her disposal. The therapist must explain to Carol how changes in cannabis use and other areas could positively affect her life. Such honest sharing may inspire trust in Carol and strengthen her willingness to engage in the process. Fears about the change process require sensitive and attentive processing. According to Miller and Rollnick, the language of honesty addresses the ambivalence within the client – between the voice supporting change and the voice opposing it (Miller & Rollnick, 2013). The therapist must listen to the reasons for the client's fears and subjective difficulties, while also addressing their hidden strengths and efforts. This approach will evoke feelings of understanding, recognition, and appreciation, encouraging the client to move forward in the process (Eliot et al., 2004; Hohman, 2012; Tudor & Merry, 2006). The therapeutic conversation with Ken demonstrates the application of the language of honesty.

Ken, thirty-three years old, slouches in the therapy chair, his face dull and tired. He's been using heroin for five years, and before that, he was addicted to alcohol. "I've already tried everything," he says quietly to the therapist, "I tried for ten years. I was in all kinds of programs, outpatient, and inpatient, but nothing worked." In recent years, he tells her, he's felt an increasing dependence on substances and now he's depressed and frustrated. During the sessions, Ken appears sad and lacking in vitality. In one session, he shared that he left his home a few days ago, but throughout the conversation, his eyes remained fixed on the floor, and he avoided talking about it. The therapist leans forward slightly and says gently, " Ken, I notice you're especially withdrawn today. When we try to talk about how you're feeling, especially about leaving

your home last week, it's not really working. Can you share it with me? What made you choose to disconnect?"
Ken does not raise his eyes. "Right," he says in a broken voice, "I'm going through some tough things. I really don't know what to do..."
"I want to honestly address what I'm hearing from you," the therapist says. "I hear two voices in you. On one hand, you want to make a significant change this time, and I believe you have the strength and ability for that change. On the other hand, I hear pessimism, despair, and maybe even fear. You don't believe anything can change – not in stopping substance use or in building a different relationship with your family."
She pauses for a moment, letting the words sink in, and continues, "I feel there's a deep lack of self-trust in you, and that lack of trust may be connected to the messages you received in childhood. You mentioned that people told you that you wouldn't succeed, that you wouldn't make it. Am I understanding correctly? Do those messages still echo for you?"

The therapist's honest approach toward Ken included reflecting on his situation and expressing trust in his ability to change. She presented to him the two internal voices he carries: on one side, the feelings of anxiety and insecurity about his ability to change, and on the other, the feelings of capability and strength that allow him to envision true change. Special emphasis was placed on strengthening the voice expressing strong feelings such as a sense of worth and confidence, while also guiding Ken to identify the defense mechanisms preventing him from believing in his ability to meet his own and the therapist's expectations (Agosta, 2020). A fundamental principle in using the language of honesty in emotion-focused interpersonal therapy is to strengthen the client's ability to honestly address their internal experiences and emotional struggles. This honesty involves confronting their personal difficulties, behavioral patterns, and substance use (Kocsis & Yellowlees, 2018). Authentic and exposed acknowledgment of emotional and behavioral difficulties allows the client to gain insights into the background and reasons for their struggles. This understanding opens up possibilities for finding suitable and effective coping strategies. An example of this comes to light in the therapeutic conversation with Roy.

Roy, a forty-eight-year-old man, enters the first session with a tense expression. For eighteen years, he's been struggling with addiction to legal and illegal gambling. "I've accumulated enormous debts," he admits quietly, "I even had to mortgage some of my family's assets."
Roy explains that his behavior has led to many family crises, and at certain times, he was forced to leave home.
Three years ago, he managed to stop gambling.
"I held on," he sighs, "but three months ago, I started gambling online again. It started because of a financial crisis I went through, and it just swept me back in."
Roy comes to therapy under heavy family pressure. During the conversation, the therapist tries to connect him with his deeper feelings and help him cope with the shame, guilt, and anxiety that are evident in him.
"In the end," Roy says, trying to sound determined, "I

believe my return to gambling is just a small glitch. I plan to quit for good this time. I don't know what happened to me, but I'm sure I can make this change."

The therapist looks at him for several moments. " Roy," he says finally, "I want to be honest with you. I don't really hear the voice supporting change in you, at least not the way you describe it. I feel you're very ashamed after your family's harsh reactions to your return to gambling. Could it be that your difficulty talking about what you really feel – the sadness and despair – comes from not truly believing in your ability to change? Can you share with me?"

Roy appears tense and moves uncomfortably in his seat. "I can change," he says almost in a whisper, "I really want to. But every time... every time something pulls me back. The environment I live in, the financial situation of me and my family... everything is so difficult. In the end, gambling is like a way to survive. It's just what I know how to do."

"I hear your fear, Roy," says the therapist, "You're afraid you'll fail again in making a change. I can understand how frustrating it must be to feel that the changes you make are temporary, and how scary the thought is that you'll disconnect again from your wife and children. But I also see strength and self-belief in you – the same strength you proved before when you fought and succeeded. I believe you have the power to make a real change."

Roy raises his eyes to the therapist, and something softens in his expression. The therapist adds, "Let's try to understand together what's stopping you from changing. I think there are emotional parts, maybe deep feelings of sadness, that you're not talking about, and that help keep you in this vicious cycle. What do you think? Would you like to join a therapeutic process that might help break the cycle you're trapped in and create change?"

The conversation with Roy highlights the core of the language of honesty in therapy: reflecting on maladaptive emotional and behavioral patterns, while providing a safe foundation, support, and an empathetic focus on the patient's internal strengths that can drive change (Johnson, 2009). When patients experience difficulty addressing their experiences and emotions honestly, they may resist sharing and working collaboratively with the therapist. The therapist should avoid reacting with counter-resistance. Instead, the therapist needs to listen to the patient's complex experiences, reflect on them, and process together the difficulties and gaps (Prochaska et al., 1992). The language of honesty, beyond exposing emotions, thoughts, and behavioral patterns, also includes practical emotional and behavioral guidance to change inhibiting patterns (Connors et al., 2013). Its goal is to encourage the patient to reflect, even initially, on their actions and help them gain insights that will allow them to break free from the addiction cycle (Tudor & Meery, 2006). Through self-reflection, the therapist can help the patient understand how emotional and behavioral patterns hinder their progress. This insight opens up options for the patient to engage honestly with their experiences and make gradual changes (Marom et al., 2011; Beck, 2011). The language of honesty requires the therapist to share honest and reliable information about the therapeutic process with the patient. The therapist must prepare the patient for anticipated difficulties, obstacles that may arise, and ways to cope with them. This information should also include the risks associated with new substances, health consequences, and the implications of relapse (Cournoyer et al., 2007).

The language of honesty: therapist feedback to the patient

- "I sense that you're trying, struggling, and working hard to understand how you got to this point."
- "I'm having difficulty sensing what you're going through today. I feel like there are things you're not talking about. Can you share a bit more about what you're feeling right now?"
- "I trust you to delve deeply in our sessions into the challenges you're experiencing so that we can tackle them together."
- "I'm optimistic that you can make a change in your life."
- "I appreciate your openness, your vulnerability, and your willingness to share what's happening for you at this time."
- "There are parts of you that you're not addressing, and I believe they're contributing to the difficulty you're feeling. Would you like to discuss them?"

In conclusion, the language of honesty, which the therapist must apply throughout all stages of emotion-focused interpersonal therapy, is an inherent part of the process of advancing the patient's awareness and insight, especially when dealing with addiction. This language helps the patient understand their strengths, capabilities, challenges, the background of their difficulties, and the possible path for change. The power of the language of honesty allows individuals in severe distress to find a genuine connection with their "self" in a respectful, non-judgmental way, thus strengthening their optimism about the ability to achieve recovery and change (Hohman, 2012).

> "The patient is the one who knows the pain they are experiencing, what problems they must face, what experiences they are hiding, and which directions they must take." (Carl Rogers)

4

EMOTION-FOCUSED APPROACH

Emotion-focused therapy (EFT) is a humanistic and experiential approach aimed at transforming painful and maladaptive emotions, such as fear or shame, into adaptive emotions like a sense of competence and control. This emotional change can, in later stages, lead to behavioral change and better adaptation to life (Greenberg, 2017; Timulak & McElvaney, 2018). Emotions are innate biological processes that evolve over time. They assist humans in daily functioning, interpersonal communication, and the ability to adapt to reality and integrate into society. Emotions provide meaning to experiences, contribute to adaptation, and allow for personal correction (Greenberg, 2016). Emotions are defined as an integrative psychological state combining physiological, sensory, and neural arousal, leading to a behavioral response (Klein et al., 1986). They encompass experiences like happiness and sadness, which together form a person's emotional makeup.

Emotion-focused therapy aims to allow the patient to experience emotions "here and now" and identify core emotional pains and their sources. Its goal is to change beliefs about emotions, manage intense emotions, and give new meaning to emotional experiences. In this way, maladaptive emotions are replaced with adaptive ones that promote change (Greenberg, 2015). The approach emphasizes performing experiential-emotional tasks that assist in resolving emotional conflicts, while focusing on the adaptive role of emotions in creating a sense of value and security (Greenberg, 2015, 2016). Greenberg created a distinction between primary and secondary emotions:

- Maladaptive primary emotions: Basic emotions like sadness, insecurity, and shame, which become inhibiting due to traumatic experiences.
- Maladaptive secondary emotions: Reactions to primary emotions, such as anger and despair, which deepen the difficulty (Greenberg & Safran, 1987).

Primary emotions that were once adaptive, such as pride, can become maladaptive, like insecurity, due to experiences of harm or deprivation in childhood or adulthood (Greenberg, 2011, 2024). Thus, emotions are an integral part of self-construction and self-organization. They help a person understand their place in interpersonal relationships and identify whether these relationships are nurturing or limiting (Timulak, 2015). Greenberg emphasizes that awareness of emotional processes is key to understanding the self and changing inhibiting emotional patterns. This process is largely influenced by a person's interactions with their environment, which shape their emotional experiences and their basic emotional blueprint (Greenberg, 2011). An emotional program containing maladaptive primary and secondary emotions can sometimes emerge due to traumatic experiences or the difficulty a person has in tolerating these emotions. Lack of awareness of this program, difficulty regulating intense emotions, or denying them may lead to distress and damage interpersonal relationships and self-actualization (Greenberg, 2011).

Emotional Transformation

Emotional transformation, which is the core of the emotion-focused therapeutic approach, focuses on replacing maladaptive emotions with more adaptive and stronger emotions, such as competence and confidence. This process aims to assist patients dealing with barriers to forming interpersonal connections and to enable better adaptation and behavioral change (Greenberg, 2017). The process includes identifying the maladaptive emotions the patient is experiencing, such as fear or shame, understanding their sources, and managing these emotions. In addition, a new narrative is created that gives a different meaning to emotional experiences, while maladaptive emotions are replaced with more adaptive ones (Greenberg, 2015).

Mechanisms of Transformation

Emotional transformation is achieved through three main stages:

1. Identifying an unmet emotion: Understanding an emotional need that is unfulfilled, such as a lack of security or love.
2. Emotional expression: Encouraging the patient to express this emotion to the therapist.

3. Creating a new narrative: Identifying positive emotional experiences from the past and giving validity and meaning to these experiences in the present, so that they can serve as an emotional alternative to unmet needs (Timulak, 2015; Shabi, 2024).

For example, fear can be replaced with a sense of security, and anger can be transformed into control. By identifying a positive emotion that was once considered adaptive, the emotional pattern of the patient can be restructured (Greenberg, 2024).

Therapeutic Alliance and Unconditional Support

A strong therapeutic alliance between the therapist and the patient is a crucial condition for the success of emotional transformation. This alliance provides a safe base for the patient, a sense of unconditional support, and trust in the therapeutic process (Brubacher, 2017). Meaningful interpersonal relationships are an integral part of working with individuals in severe distress, enabling the patient to feel understood and accepted (Cassidy & Shaver, 2016).

Emotional Validation and Reflection of Feelings

Emotional validation serves as an important tool in transformation. The therapist seeks to deeply and authentically understand the patient's feelings (such as unconscious anxiety) and reflects them back to the patient. This process allows the patient to view their experiences in a new light, identify active defense mechanisms, and regulate maladaptive emotions (Lafrance et al., 2020). Emotional validation helps patients recognize the hidden reasons behind their emotional denial, such as pain stemming from addiction. It opens a way for them to process painful emotions, often for the first time, and lays the groundwork for significant emotional change (Elliott, 2004).

Summary

The emotion-focused therapeutic approach, with emotional transformation at its core, describes a deep and reflective process that combines identifying maladaptive emotions, managing and expressing emotions, and constructing a new narrative for emotional experiences. Through emotional validation and reflection of feelings, the therapist helps the patient deal with painful core emotions, and create emotional change that leads to behavioral and adaptive improvement. The approach emphasizes the importance of the therapeutic alliance and the authentic connection between therapist and patient as a means of creating a secure and strengthening foundation for change.

> "Life is illogical without the existence of an interpersonal connection. We need each other, and the sooner we learn this, the better for all of us" (Erikson).

5

EMOTION-FOCUSED THERAPY: CLINICAL TASKS

In the initial stages of Emotion-Focused Therapy (EFT), the main task is to help the patient examine themselves, identify the central pain they are experiencing, and understand the background of these feelings. Even in these early stages, the patient should be given the opportunity to express emotions such as pain and anxiety, alongside assistance in moderating intense emotions they tend to avoid "meeting" in daily life. These emotions, such as feelings of rejection or shame, may stem from early experiences of harm or trauma.

Emotional Transformation focuses on replacing maladaptive emotions with stronger and more adaptive emotions. For example, a person dealing with a sense of helplessness in stopping substance use, despite their desire to do so, may undergo an emotional shift. Through participation in a long-term therapeutic program, the feeling of helplessness can be replaced by a strong sense of competence and control. Emotional transformation brings to awareness, for example, the sense of failure in establishing a healthy family life due to addiction issues — and replaces it with a feeling of trust in the patient's ability to repair their family. This shift is made through a combination of emotional, cognitive, and behavioral elements, along with the creation of a new emotional narrative that emphasizes feelings of control, strength, and security.

Emotion-Focused Therapy: The Flow Process

According to Greenberg (2015), the emotional change process in Emotion-Focused Therapy consists of six stages, focusing on corrective emotional experiences and emotional transformation. In the research underlying this book, particular emphasis is placed on the emotional change during the flow process, which involves replacing automatic maladaptive emotions with positive and adaptive ones — a vital step for maintaining and internalizing emotional change, and in a later stage, behavioral change (Shabi, 2024), particularly for populations dealing with distress and addiction.

Stage One: Awareness

This stage focuses on deepening the awareness of the patient suffering from addiction, including strengthening their understanding of passive emotions such as sadness and insecurity, and enhancing their ability to feel these emotions. It includes:

- Interpersonal intervention will enhance the patient's ability to be aware of hidden primary emotions and express them.
- Managing secondary emotions such as anger and despair, which obscure other emotions, processing these emotions, and addressing them.
- A joint assessment with the patient regarding the

hidden and overt reasons for repressing primary emotions.
- Strengthening the patient's ability to express positive, hidden emotions such as control and self-confidence (Greenberg, 2010).

Stage Two: Enhancing the Ability to Experience Emotion

In this stage, the therapist helps the patient dealing with addiction understand the source of their maladaptive secondary emotions. This stage involves:

- Examining doubts, the patient has regarding their ability to cope with substance use issues and their fears related to changing addictive patterns.
- Promoting the patient's ability to gain insights and recognize the strong emotions within themselves, such as a sense of value and strength, indicating their true capabilities (Goldman et al., 2021).
- Assisting the patient in listening to emotions they have not been able to "hear" until now, such as sadness and shame (Greenberg, 2024).

Stage Three: Emotion Regulation

This stage focuses on enhancing the ability of patients experiencing intense emotions, such as anger and rage, to process and control them within the therapeutic process. The stage includes:

- A joint examination with the patient of experiences and events they were previously involved in, in which they experienced fear, anger, tension, and helplessness.
- Identifying the type of emotion, the patient is experiencing in different events: primary emotions such as sadness, or secondary emotions such as despair.
- Quantifying and processing primary emotions, including insecurity related to difficulties in changing addiction-related patterns and behaviors, as well as secondary emotions such as confusion from substance use that alters consciousness. The primary and secondary emotions are presented in proportion to the reality of their life context.
- Focusing the patient's attention on emotions like loneliness and fear that contributed to long-term dependence on substances, and presenting alternative emotions, such as confidence and competence (Greenberg, 2010).
- Strengthening the patient's ability to independently regulate and manage emotions through relaxation methods and techniques, including mindfulness techniques. This involves practicing meditation, where the patient focuses on emotions of value and control, purposefully and non-judgmentally directing attention to physical sensations, such as breath or parts of the body, and observing emotional experiences within them. This process allows the patient to "watch

from the side" passing thoughts and quiet them, as well as observe external experiences — events in the immediate environment they were involved (Micheli et al., 2016).

Stage Four: Reflection

In this stage, the therapist reflects back to the patient dealing with addiction the emotions they are experiencing, in order to deepen their understanding of existing emotional patterns and create new narratives. The stage includes:

- Assisting the patient in turning inward and examining their emotions while developing a critical perspective and self-feedback on negative emotional experiences they carry, such as self-disappointment due to the difficulty in disconnecting from the world of drugs.
- Strengthening the patient's learning ability and awareness of the "self" and taking responsibility for patterns of lack of control, violence, and self-anger.
- Deepening the patient's awareness of their emotions and reducing the use of mechanisms of emotion denial (Greenberg, 2015).
- Identifying positive emotions that were previously dismissed by the patient, such as a sense of control and competence, and bringing them to the forefront emotionally, with the aim of strengthening their belief in their ability to change

and alter the emotions they experience on a daily basis.

Stage Five: Emotion Transformation

This stage involves converting primary emotions, such as sadness and insecurity, and secondary emotions, such as despair and anger, into other positive emotions like competence, control, and self-worth (Greenberg, 2010). This stage includes:

- Strengthening the ability of the patient dealing with addiction to recognize the variety of maladaptive feelings they experience, such as shame and pessimism, and how these emotions affect their life (Greenberg, 2015, 2024).
- Joint processing with the patient of maladaptive emotions, such as hopelessness regarding breaking free from the addiction cycle, including a detailed analysis of past and present events and experiences that are etched in their memory.
- Converting maladaptive emotions, such as anger, into strong feelings of self-trust and the ability to change by increasing the patient's awareness of positive emotions they've experienced in the past, such as confidence, and reinforcing their ability to "store" new information about these emotions and change negative memories.
- Cognitive integration of strong, adaptive emotions in an individual dealing with addiction, such as a sense of control, through emotional

assessment processes, and reinforcing this integration by reflecting on how these emotions manifest in their current emotional reality. The cognitive integration process includes:

- Identifying the connection between emotions and thoughts and understanding the mechanisms that led the patient to distance themselves from adaptive emotions and thoughts, such as optimism and the ability to cope effectively with addiction problems.
- Examining and assessing negative thinking patterns, such as "I am helpless," and "I have no control over my drinking," and collectively evaluating the connection between these thoughts and reality.
- Identifying alternative thoughts and building a new narrative that emphasizes the patient's strengths and capabilities, such as "I am responsible," and "I can change" (Aharonovich et al., 2018).
- Assessing the importance of positive thoughts, identifying events that illustrate a new perspective on reality, and strengthening the patient's ability to draw more adaptive conclusions about their abilities to break free from addiction, reduce substance use, and sever harmful interpersonal relationships (Marom et al., 2011).
- Converting automatic negative and maladaptive thoughts, such as "I'm a failure," "I'll never stop smoking cannabis," or "I

disappoint myself and those around me," into positive thoughts based on past successes, such as "I reduced my substance use before," "I made the decision to change and I stuck with it," "I can persist in stopping gambling behavior" (Beck, 2011).
    - Deepening awareness of mental filtering processes of emotions, leads to changes in behavioral patterns, reducing dependence on mood-altering substances, and reinforcing the patient's sense of control and competence (Aharonovich et al., 2018).

Stage Six: Corrective Emotional Experience

This stage focuses on transforming one emotion into another within the interpersonal relationship between the therapist and the patient dealing with addiction. The stage includes:

- Strengthening the patient's ability to express new, positive emotions to the therapist, such as assertiveness and trust in their ability to adapt to reality. These new emotions will replace the corresponding negative emotions they carry, such as insecurity and despair (Greenberg, 2024).
- Encouraging the patient to express strong positive emotions, demonstrating that they have acquired the language of emotional change (Hohama, 2012), and integrating these into a new narrative (Greenberg & Elliott, 1996), where pride, self-

worth, and a sense of competence are at the forefront.

- Strengthening the patient's ability to understand their inner world and experience positive emotions that are attuned to reality (Connors et al., 2013).

The clinical activity, including emotional transformation, corrective emotional experience, and cognitive integration, is illustrated in a section from a therapeutic conversation with steven, a person struggling with a gambling addiction.

Steven, a 45-year-old man, married with three grown children, works in sales. In the last two and a half years, he began gambling online, mostly on blackjack games, in an uncontrolled manner. At first, he gambled without money but later started investing a hundred dollars every evening, and in the past year, the amounts reached hundreds of dollars almost daily.

In a session with the therapist, Steven shares that he is shocked by the situation he has found himself in: "I never thought I'd end up like this," he says. "I can't leave the computer or phone, and all day I think about gambling." He mentions that in the past, he was able to stop gambling for four months, but returned to the world of gambling.

The situation worsened significantly after his wife discovered that there was no money in their bank account and that they had accumulated debts of two hundred thousand dollars. She gave him an ultimatum: treat the addiction problem or leave the house. Although he is still living at home, Steven describes a painful disconnect between him and his wife in recent months.

Steven came to therapy without a genuine desire: "I don't see myself as an addict like others here," he says to the therapist. "I believe I can stop on my own." However, during the sessions, he appears blocked and weary, often expressing frustration and disappointment with himself and his situation.

The therapist gently responds, "I feel the sadness and pain you're experiencing, the inability to stop gambling, and the disconnect from your family. It's hard for you to talk about what you're going through, about your emotions right now. Am I understanding this correctly?"

Steven nods. "That's right, that's me. I don't talk about emotions, not even with my wife. But I can tell you, I'm disappointed in myself. I don't understand how I fell into this. It was once 'just a little,' but now... debts, distance from the family... it's a nightmare."

The therapist softly asks, "Can you look back a little? What keeps you from talking about things? What's stopping you?"

Steven pauses and responds, "I think it's related to my father. All these years, it was hard for me with him. He belittled me, and humiliated me. I tried to get close, but it never worked. I haven't spoken to him in many years. It held me back in life – I dropped out of the army, and worked odd jobs, and it came to nothing. The gambling, weirdly, gave me energy, but it's clear it's temporary – with it comes the price."

The therapist listens attentively. "I feel that the loneliness, insecurity, and shame you're experiencing stem from the hurts you suffered in your relationship with your father. These are feelings that have been with you until today and have a significant impact on you. I'm wondering – do you think the gambling really compensates for these feelings, or does it just intensify your frustration and pessimism?"

Steven looks at her and remains silent.

"I think," the therapist continues, "that here, in our treatment, there is an opportunity for you. An opportunity to reflect on your experiences in a new way, to understand the emotions that shape your life, and to change some of them to emotions of control and confidence. This could lead to a renewed connection with your family and your wife, and also to dealing with the gambling problem differently. You've done it before – you stopped gambling for a period, and you showed responsibility toward your family. You have strength, and I believe you can do it again."

Focused Emotional Therapy: Complementary Clinical Tasks

Greenberg, Timulak, and other researchers have presented clinical stages intended for the practical application of the emotional transformation process in patients. These stages focus on processing core pains, developing self-soothing processes, and using therapeutic tools tailored to working with populations dealing with addiction (Timulak & McElvaney, 2018; Micheli et al., 2016).

Core Pain Processing

1. Guiding the Patient to Expose Core Pains: The patient struggling with addiction is guided to reveal the core pains they experience, such as loneliness, shame, and fear, and to confront them while identifying the factors that contributed to their development (Greenberg, 2024).
2. Deepening Memories Related to Core Pain: Delving into memories associated with the central emotional pain the patient feels, such as events that caused sadness or helplessness, and examining their context.
3. Identifying and Processing Unclear Physical Sensations: Identifying and processing bodily sensations that the patient may not understand but are related to deep emotional pain, such as loneliness stemming from experiences of humiliation or abuse.
4. Inviting the Patient to Describe Physical Sensations in the Present: Encouraging the patient to describe the physical sensations they experience during moments of emotional pain in the here and now, and to see the connection between those physical feelings and the emotional experience.
5. Encouraging the Expression of Pain from Rejection or Neglect: Encouraging the patient to express the pain caused by feelings of rejection or neglect, while helping them cope with the tendency to avoid expressing these emotions.

6. Fostering Self-Compassion: Encouraging the patient to develop compassion for themselves and to recognize the missed opportunities they've experienced in life due to long-term substance use, alongside cultivating pride for their strengths and achievements.
7. Joint Processing of the Need to Be Loved, Accepted, and Protected: Working with the patient to process their need to be loved, accepted, and protected, and how this unfulfilled need affects their emotions and behavior.
8. Processing Self-Criticism: Processing the self-directed criticism the patient may harbor, such as disdain or contempt, and reinforcing their ability to accept themselves, nurture a positive self-image, and take responsibility for change.
9. Working Through Unfinished Emotional Business: Addressing unfinished feelings, such as interpersonal rejection, judgment, and fear, and examining how they affect the patient's present life.
10. Developing "protective anger": Helping the patient develop protective anger that allows them to set boundaries and feel capable of defending themselves against rejection and humiliation resulting from prolonged substance use.

Self-Soothing

1. Developing the Patient's Ability to Imagine Positive Sensory Experiences: Helping the

patient develop the ability to imagine sights, sounds, and smells. The activity includes taking deep breaths, focusing on breathing, sensations, and meaningful events the patient has experienced.

2. Documenting Emotions Related to Abstinence: Encouraging the patient to record emotions such as fear and shame that are connected to the difficulty of abstaining from substance use.
3. Recording Positive Feelings of Competence and Control: Documenting strong feelings of competence and control the patient has experienced in the past week while describing how they coped with the world of addiction.
4. Imagining an Event with Maladaptive Emotions: Encouraging the patient to imagine a scenario in which they experience an unregulated emotion, like self-anger or despair, in the context of their addiction struggles.
5. Imagining an Event with Positive Emotions: Encouraging the patient to imagine a scenario in which they experience a strong positive emotion, such as self-pride or a sense of worth, indicating their ability to cope with excessive substance use.
6. Therapist-Patient Dialogue on Strong Emotions: Facilitating a conversation between the therapist and patient in which the patient expresses strong emotions and writes them down.
7. Expressing Emotional Needs: Encouraging the patient to express emotional needs they may feel are unmet, such as love and support.

8. Identifying Positive Emotions of Strength and Worth: Encouraging the patient to identify emotions that reflect they are a good or strong person, capable of facing difficulties.
9. Developing "Protective Anger" for Coping with Fear and Anxiety: Fostering "protective anger" in the patient, enabling them to confront feelings of fear and anxiety, such as statements like "I can stand up to people who disappointed me" or "I won't let them hurt me again."

Emotional Transformation Language: Therapist Feedback to the Patient

- "I want to help you reduce the guilt you're feeling and focus on the sense of control and capability you demonstrated four months ago when you tried to stay abstinent from alcohol."
- "I see that unlike in the past, in our current conversation, you are able to focus on your strength and pride, which is reflected in the process of change you've gone through."
- "Do you think your denial of the fear of failure in dealing with family issues is related to a lack of appreciation for your abilities? You've made significant progress in your ability to adapt and take responsibility within the therapeutic framework. I believe in you."
- "You're expressing anger towards the treatment team, but it might reflect anxiety about failing to adapt to the treatment plan. However, you've

already demonstrated strength and self-control in facing social difficulties within the treatment environment. I'm confident you'll overcome this obstacle too."

- "I'm wondering what's blocking you from expressing your feelings. You have a sincere desire to make a change, which is evident in the way you've cut ties with your old social circle. I'm confident you'll continue to progress as you expect."
- "You're caught between feeling hopeless about improving your relationship with your father and knowing you can solve problems and make decisions in other areas. I believe you'll overcome the current crisis and act differently this time."
- "What makes you anxious about your relationship with your partner? The history of failures in handling addiction may leave you feeling insecure, but you are not the same person. Today, you're active in social circles and seeking solutions to your difficulties. I'm optimistic about your future."
- "You speak honestly about the pain you felt from your family's neglect. However, many times you've shown determination in dealing with loneliness after your divorce. You have the strength to confront the addiction issue as well."
- "Do you think the recent disconnection is due to a lack of trust in your ability to achieve the goals you've set? I hear two inner voices in you – one for and one against change. Share with me how you're feeling."

- "I sense that you feel shame and self-anger about the difficulty of maintaining a relationship with your children, but you're making efforts to reconnect with your family. You've tried in many ways to be an involved father. This complexity doesn't diminish your trust in yourself or your optimism."
- "The decision to join a mental health treatment program is a source of pride. You've demonstrated control and responsibility, and you're making genuine changes."
- "The loneliness you feel after distancing yourself from your father is understandable, especially in light of past neglect. I empathize with your sense of insecurity, but I believe in your ability to form meaningful social connections and take control of your life."
- "I see your impressive progress in the process. You're assertive and showing excellent abilities in achieving the goals you've set for yourself in dealing with substance use. I believe in you."
- "Your sadness and anger toward your parents, who haven't been supportive, are understandable. However, you can remember your proven ability to make good decisions and create meaningful connections. I believe you'll overcome this crisis too."

"Not knowing your past means being enslaved by it: awareness of the past allows for a sense of liberation." (Freud)

6

EMOTIONAL CHANGE, BEHAVIORAL CHANGE: A SHORT-TERM EMOTION-FOCUSED TREATMENT

"I can feel guilty about my past actions and fear for the future, but only in the present I can act. The ability to experience, act, and change the present is a key component of mental health" (Maslow)

Unmet emotional needs such as self-worth, competence, and security throughout life can often lead to the development of an emotional schema that does not align with reality (Timulak, 2015). This schema is often characterized by feelings of anxiety, anger, and sadness, which frequently accompany individuals struggling with addiction over extended periods of their lives. These emotions contribute to attempts at self-healing, sometimes through excessive substance use. For individuals dealing with addiction, it is crucial to develop a personalized treatment plan that simultaneously addresses emotional challenges and the addiction itself, tailored to the unique needs of each patient. Such a plan aims to promote emotional change, encourage emotional transformation, and facilitate behavioral change, including improved functionality and reduced dependence on substances, as detailed in the chapters of this book.

This chapter presents a short-term framework for emotion-focused treatment for addiction. The framework emphasizes key intervention principles, focusing on structured therapeutic sessions. The series of sessions follow a logical progression with clearly defined clinical tasks. The sessions are held weekly, either in a clinic or a dedicated addiction treatment setting, over the course of sixteen meetings.

SHORT-TERM EMOTION-FOCUSED TREATMENT FRAMEWORK

Building Rapport and Establishing an Interpersonal Relationship

During these sessions, the therapist provides the patient with information about the emotion-focused therapeutic approach, the phenomenon of substance use, and addictive behavior. An initial assessment of the patient's condition and primary substance-related issues is conducted. Additionally, the therapist offers practical assistance with immediate concerns occupying the patient, such as medical issues, employment, housing, or navigating their rights. The therapist and patient discuss treatment goals, both in the emotional domain and regarding excessive substance use and addictive behaviors. Emphasis is placed on creating a personal connection, building initial trust, reducing feelings of helplessness, and fostering positive expectations about the patient's ability to achieve emotional change and alter substance-related patterns.

This stage usually spans two sessions.

Addiction Assessment

The diagnostic process aims to establish a direct and authentic connection with the prospective patient and build a therapeutic alliance based on collaboration in shaping the treatment process while understanding the patient's strengths and capacity for change (Gibson, 2011). The assessment is not limited to an objective observation but also involves an interpersonal and emotional learning process (Shabi, 2023) aimed at understanding the patient's personal, emotional, and cognitive characteristics. The process focuses on understanding the patient's present behavior and analyzing the familial and environmental influences on their overall functioning (Roger, 1951; Yalom, 2019). In emotion-focused assessment, attention is directed toward understanding the patient's deep emotions, the etiological factors leading to the addiction, and the emotional background underlying their feelings. The following excerpt from an introductory session with Bruce illustrates this approach:

Bruce sits heavily in the chair across from the therapist, avoiding eye contact.
The therapist begins, "I must say that even in the short time we've known each other, I can sense the sadness and disappointment you're feeling about not being able to stop drinking. I'm listening to you and the criticism you have about the treatment system. I hope you'll give me the chance to get to know you better and understand what is truly preventing you from confronting this issue."
Bruce slowly nods his head. "It's not that I haven't tried,"

he says in a low voice, almost apologetically. "I've already been in a few treatment programs. I tried to explain to the therapists what I was going through, what was hard for me, but… I guess I couldn't. There are so many things I can't seem to resolve. I really don't understand why I can't stop drinking. Maybe you'll be able to figure it out."

"Bruce" the therapist responds, "from what you've shared with me so far, I believe there's room to talk about topics you may not have addressed before. Perhaps this could be an opportunity to make a significant step forward. For example, we could discuss the events that led to your estrangement from your mother—the guilt and distress you're feeling because of them. I believe that talking about it could help ease some of the burden you're carrying."

Bruce remains silent, seemingly lost in thought. The therapist continues, "From my understanding, as part of our work together, we can explore the barriers that are preventing you from confronting your drinking. It will be a therapeutic journey, but one I believe you're capable of undertaking. Are you willing to participate in this process?"

The diagnostic process, as illustrated in Bruce case, aims to provide the patient with an opportunity to understand the deep-seated reasons for the obstacles they have faced in their attempts to change. The process relies on empathetic emotional inquiry, encouraging the patient to share their emotional experiences—both primary and secondary—without reservation (Greenberg, 2015). The assessment helps identify painful core emotions, such as despair, which may contribute to emotional and behavioral blocks (Elliott, 2004). As part of the assessment, the therapist conveys a message of unconditional acceptance while working with the patient to understand the emotional narrative behind their struggles. The process addresses the patient's avoidance of their emotions, such as fear and pessimism, and examines how these feelings impact their daily functioning (Greenberg, 2010).

Stages of the Assessment

Personal History and Daily Functioning

The therapist inquires about the patient's personal history, crises they have experienced, and the connection between these events and their current difficulties. The patient is invited to openly and nonjudgmentally share their coping strategies for addiction, their capacity for change, and the personal and environmental barriers they have encountered. The assessment also includes an overview of the patient's daily activities, such as education, work, and leisure, and an attempt to understand their significance for the patient. Additionally, the therapist examines the characteristics of the patient's interpersonal relationships, including their use of social media and the frequency of their substance and alcohol consumption. The goal is to map emotional and behavioral patterns in daily life that deepen barriers to change (Hohman, 2012).

Information from External Sources

With the patient's consent, the therapist may obtain reports and psychosocial information from sources the patient has been involved with in the past. Additionally, meetings with family members, friends, acquaintances, and even the patient's employer may provide valuable insights into the patient's unique emotional and behavioral characteristics. This information allows the therapist to identify both overt and hidden strengths in the patient and to reinforce them (Sanders, 2000). However, while meetings with family members can provide important perspectives, caution must be exercised to avoid inaccurate interpretations. Family members of individuals struggling with addiction often face their own difficulties or distress, including addiction, which may influence how they portray the patient. They may deny, minimize, or exaggerate the patient's addiction issues, making the information they provide partial or unreliable (Sanders, 2000). According to Tombs (2005), family members may engage in a "code of silence" around the patient's addiction, sometimes due to disappointment that the patient has not succeeded in recovery over the years. A professional therapist must acknowledge these attitudes and identify pathological family dynamics (homeostasis), where family members resist change or the therapeutic process to maintain the current status quo. At times, family members may downplay the significance of the changes the patient seeks to make, emphasizing the difficulties they have observed over the years. When authentic information cannot be obtained from family members, healthcare and community resources may be consulted in coordination with the patient.

Despite these complexities, engaging with family members remains highly valuable. It broadens the emotional and behavioral understanding of the patient and highlights problematic family patterns that affect their functioning. Including the family in the diagnostic and therapeutic process can empower the patient and support the changes they aim to achieve (Connors et al., 2013).

Practical Support

During the assessment phase, it is crucial to provide the patient with practical support in accessing rights and resolving issues related to employment, housing, and financial debts. This support is not only practical but also emotional, strengthening the interpersonal connection between the therapist and the patient and increasing the patient's willingness to participate in the therapeutic process (Flores, 2004; Hohman, 2012).

Assessing Substance Dependence

The assessment should focus on the patient's level of substance dependence, usage patterns, frequency, and the emotional and functional implications of their addiction. Tools such as the "Assist" and the "ASI", known for their reliability in mapping addiction patterns and assessing key areas of the patient's life—including family functioning, mental health, and occupational performance—are often utilized (WHO, 2010; SAMHSA, 2013). Drug and alcohol testing during the assessment or treatment phase remains a controversial issue. On the one hand, testing provides clarity regarding the patient's condition. On the other hand, it can provoke anxiety and fear in the patient, potentially undermining interpersonal connection and trust. Many therapists prefer to rely on the patient's self-reports to maintain an atmosphere of respect and trust.

As one therapist described: "These tests create unnecessary tension and shift the focus from trust-related issues to bureaucracy. They undermine the opportunity to build a meaningful therapeutic relationship." A segment from a therapeutic conversation with Jason illustrates the dilemmas surrounding the issue of monitoring psychoactive substances and their impact on the therapeutic process.

Jason, a 27-year-old, sits in the therapy room in yet another attempt to understand himself and his situation. For the past four years, he has used cocaine—a substance he began consuming during social gatherings. He shares with the therapist the sense of liberation the substance provided him but also the emotional toll he is paying: sadness, anxiety, and deep disappointment in himself. "At first, it made me feel good, even amazing," he says, "but now I feel like I've lost control. I've tried to quit three times on my own. Each time ended the same way—going back to using."

The therapist listens empathetically. "I hear that you've made significant efforts to stop using," she says. "But I also hear your fear—the fear of not being able to manage feelings like the sadness and anxiety you're describing. Those feelings can be very confusing. I sense you're also angry with yourself, maybe because you couldn't stop as you'd hoped."

Jason nods slowly, his eyes reflecting sadness.

The therapist continues, "But I also see something else in you—the strength it takes to talk about this, the willingness to look inward and try to understand. That's no small thing. It's a significant and important step. I believe that to move forward, we first need to understand the background of these feelings and create a plan together. The plan will focus not only on changing your patterns of cocaine use but also on addressing the emotional experiences that surface for you."

Jason looks worried. "But what about the drug monitoring tests you do here?" he asks. "They stress me out."

The therapist smiles gently. "I understand your concern," she says, "but I want to clarify that you're not required to take such tests here with us. I trust you to share if there's a relapse into cocaine or other substance use. Our goal is not to create pressure but to create a space where you feel safe to talk about everything you're experiencing."

She pauses briefly, giving Jason time to process her words. "I truly believe this could be an opportunity for change for you," she adds. "Would you like to join the treatment here at the center?"

The conversation with Jason highlights the principles of emotionally focused interpersonal interventions, where a clear message is conveyed to the client: the therapist sees them as honest, responsible, and capable of self-regulation. Building such a supportive connection encourages clients to openly share their experiences, including relapses into substance use, and seek help in addressing them. Trusting the client is not only a sign of respect but also a tool that enhances their sense of personal responsibility and motivation for emotional and behavioral change (Tudor & Meery, 2006; Wachtel, P.L., 1993).

Emotional Assessment

The emotional assessment process focuses on identifying and understanding unclear aspects of the client's emotional narrative. The therapist seeks to uncover the sources of emotional denial or the inability to fully experience emotions. The emotional assessment process is based on identifying primary emotions expressed by the client, such as immediate feelings like sadness, and secondary emotions, which are reactions to other emotions, such as despair stemming from insecurity. Accurate identification of these emotional types is critical for the diagnostic process. For instance, an emotion like shame may appear as both a primary and a secondary emotion, necessitating a deeper exploration of the context in which it arises (Timulak & Mcelvaney, 2018). Maladaptive primary emotions, which emerge from traumatic experiences such as rejection by significant attachment figures, may lead to low self-esteem (Greenberg, 2017, 2024). These feelings—such as hopelessness and helplessness—become embedded in the client's emotional memory, forming a recurring emotional pattern. The assessment process emphasizes gaining insights into how this pattern manifests and influences the client's self-confidence and social standing.

The therapist seeks to help the client identify core emotional pain points and understand their connection to everyday behaviors. The process also examines passive emotions within the client and distinguishes between secondary emotions, such as anger, and underlying primary emotions, such as sadness. Effective emotional assessment enables the client to comprehend the root causes of their struggles, listen to their emotions, and recognize initial ways to address them within an emotionally focused therapy framework (Greenberg, 2015). The findings from the assessment and the intervention plan are presented to the client and documented in their treatment record.

Typically, the assessment stage takes place over two sessions.

MOTIVATIONAL ENGAGEMENT FOR EMOTIONAL CHANGE

Ruth, a 26-year-old woman, has been struggling with prescription drug addiction for approximately five years. She was referred to treatment by her general practitioner. During her meeting with the therapist, Ruth openly admits that she has low motivation to engage in the process. "I don't really have a problem," she says, adding that the idea of treating herself feels strange to her. However, the therapist senses that Ruth is in distress and in need of help.

One of the central questions in the therapeutic process is how to motivate individuals like Ruth, who have low levels of motivation, to consider the possibility of receiving focused emotional support. The motivational interviewing approach, introduced by Miller and Rollnick, provides tools that enable clients to build confidence and the capacity to change (Miller & Rollnick, 2002). This approach emphasizes interpersonal relationships as the foundation for the change process, similar to the emotion-focused approach, and can be applied at various stages of therapy. It strengthens emotional, cognitive, and behavioral processes. The use of empathy, support, and acceptance can encourage the client and increase their willingness to engage in therapy (Miller & Rollnick, 2002).

The Motivational Interviewing Approach

Motivational interviewing involves the use of an ongoing therapeutic dialogue that delves into the language of change. This dialogue helps the client understand the significance of personal change and enhances their confidence in their ability to achieve it. The therapist identifies the client's core emotions, such as anger or insecurity, and employs reflective listening that highlights their strengths and positive resources (Miller & Moyers, 2017).

Motivational Challenges Among Individuals with Addictions

Research has shown that individuals who use psychoactive substances as a defense mechanism against traumatic experiences often exhibit low motivation to engage in treatments aimed at reducing or ceasing substance use. For many, substances serve as a "shield" against emotions like fear and sadness (Sanders, 2000; Shabi, 2023). In the past, certain therapeutic approaches emphasized direct confrontation with these behavioral patterns and placed the therapist's authority at the center. However, this method is inconsistent with the principles of motivational interviewing. Instead, this approach focuses on empowering the client through emotional support and collaborative relationships (Deleon, 2010). In the context of emotion-focused therapy, the therapist and client explore ambivalence surrounding change together. Clients are encouraged to express both their reasons for change and the obstacles preventing it (Miller & Rollnick, 2013). Rosengren (2018) highlights that shifting the traditional dynamic between therapist and client—where the therapist encourages change and the client resists it—can help overcome this ambivalence. The therapist assists the client in identifying both subjective and objective factors hindering change, such as the client's feelings of shame or positive pressure from family members.

Reflection as a Tool for Facilitating Change

Miller and Rollnick (2013) describe three types of reflection that promote change:

1. Simple Reflection: Paraphrasing the client's words, e.g., "You're feeling guilt and confusion about not succeeding in stopping your drinking. Am I understanding you correctly?"
2. Complex Reflection: The therapist highlights the underlying meaning behind the client's words, e.g., "Could it be that the loneliness you've felt since your wife left is connected to the passivity you're showing in therapy sessions?"
3. Expanded Reflection: Presenting the client's ambivalence and summarizing the process thus

far, e.g., "I sense that you're avoiding addressing your anxiety and lack of self-confidence, which are making it hard for you to decide to join a rehabilitation program. What do you think?"

Open Questions and Dialogical Process

Rosengren (2018) recommends using open-ended questions that deepen the therapist's understanding of the meaning the client attributes to change. For example:

- "How do you see the differences between your life in the past and what you're experiencing now?"
- "What keeps you in your current situation, despite the difficulties you've described?"

An open dialogue, accompanied by optimism and belief in the client's strengths, enables the therapist and the client to jointly explore the potential for change.

Setting Clear Goals and Creating Cognitive Dissonance

One method to motivate change involves setting concrete goals, such as reducing feelings of loneliness, framed in the present tense. The therapist helps the client process the gap between their current behavior (e.g., substance use) and their aspirations (e.g., responsible living without substances). This processing, known as cognitive dissonance, serves as a key tool for enhancing motivation for change. Hettema (2009) describes how unconscious cognitive mechanisms, such as avoidance of thoughts or patterns, can prevent clients from recognizing inconsistencies in their behavior. This lack of awareness often leaves the client resistant to change. Strengthening the client's awareness of these mechanisms, which are often rooted in traumatic experiences, can be pivotal in fostering change. For instance, the therapist may use reflective listening to explore feelings of disappointment, sadness, and helplessness stemming from memories of humiliation or abuse. They might identify maladaptive beliefs, such as perceived inadequacy compared to others' abilities. By presenting alternative, positive perspectives, the therapist helps the client reconstruct their personal narrative, integrating emotions and thoughts that emphasize confidence and self-efficacy.

The patient's strengths as a means of encouraging change

Rosengren and Apodaca et al. (2015, 2018) emphasize the importance of highlighting the client's positive traits and strengths. Rather than focusing on analyzing past decisions and their outcomes, this approach prioritizes the client's initial reflections on change. Connecting with these strengths enables the client to reconsider their resistance and explore new coping strategies.

External Support and Integrated Motivation

Loke and Schattke (2018) highlight the significant impact of external influences, such as family members, law enforcement, and community involvement. These influences can assist clients in making short-term changes when combined with existing internal motivation. This integrated approach allows even clients in severe distress to overcome personal barriers.

Intervention Processes for Change

1. Pre-Contemplation

Clients struggling with addiction may experience a "pre-contemplation" stage, where they do not actively reflect on the need to reduce or cease substance use (Miller & Rollnick, 2002). For many, psychoactive substances are perceived as a "medication" that alleviates traumatic experiences. In this stage, fear of giving up these substances may leave clients feeling helpless and at an increased risk.

- **Contemplation**

At this stage, the therapist guides the client through a process of self-reflection, focusing on significant emotional experiences such as anger or pain. This reflection helps clients re-evaluate their priorities. Therapists might ask questions such as: "What place does your family, health, and substance use hold in your life? Is it time to reconsider your priorities?"

2. Motivation Building

This stage involves fostering the client's internal motivation for change. The goal is to strengthen the client's determination, willingness, and persistence in making changes while improving their functioning and social adaptation. In this therapeutic process, emphasizing the client's autonomy is crucial. The therapist enables the client to independently decide whether to engage in treatment and set their own change goals. This approach supports the client in bringing their "authentic self" into the therapeutic dialogue (Miller & Moyars, 2017). The change process does not necessarily require setting specific goals, such as a target date for cessation of use. Instead, it focuses on enhancing the client's self-worth and confidence, which will ultimately empower them to define their personal goals (Naar & Safren, 2017; Zuckoff, 2001).

Conclusion: The Client Drives the Change Process

Motivational interviewing emphasizes exploring the client's ambivalence and identifying internal reasons that either hinder or support the change process. To achieve this, the therapist creates a supportive environment where the client feels safe to express their emotions and thoughts. This process involves strengthening the client's ability to express commitment and insight into change while emphasizing the potential for personal recovery and functional improvement. This approach minimizes resistance to change, cultivates a "language of change" and commitment, and reinforces the client's desire and ability to achieve change (Rosengren, 2018). The therapist helps the client envision what their future might look like after the change, encouraging them to recognize the positive impacts on their health, functioning, and overall well-being. The motivational interviewing approach offers a holistic framework that focuses on both enhancing internal motivation and utilizing external support. It views the client as an active partner, leading the change process and building confidence in their abilities. By integrating the described tools and stages, therapists and clients can collaboratively work toward recovery, growth, and improved quality of life.

This stage typically spans two sessions.

Interpersonal Intervention

The Language of Empathy

The use of active and interpretive empathy language is a key component of the therapeutic process, both in the early stages of emotion-focused therapy and throughout it. This language is based on an interpersonal dialogue between the therapist and the patient, emphasizing recognition, support, and strengthening the patient's awareness of their adaptive and maladaptive emotions, without judgment or negative evaluation (Agosta, 2010, 2015). Active empathy language involves, on one hand, deep identification with the addiction sufferer's challenging feelings and experiences, and on the other, expanding their awareness of the background leading to their maladaptive emotions (Jacobs, 2013). Empathic interpretation encourages the patient to express their feelings within the therapy, promotes insights into inhibiting emotional patterns, and enables processing and analysis of the background to hidden feelings that do not contribute to progress (Agosta, 2015).

Unconditional Support Language

Unconditional support language focuses on active actions from the therapist, including expressing positive feelings toward the patient, encouragement, care, and reinforcing the patient's achievements, both small and large, as well as highlighting and revealing their hidden and visible strengths that encourage personal change. The main goal of support language is to make the patient feel important, desirable, loved, and accepted. Through this approach, the therapist encourages the patient to believe in their own strength, ability, and capacity to deal with their maladaptive emotions, functional difficulties, and addiction, here and now (Greenman & Johnson, 2022).

These last two steps typically occur over two sessions.

Emotional Transformation Activation

This phase of the therapeutic intervention aims to enhance the ability of the patient struggling with addiction to regulate and soften maladaptive emotions. The main goal is to help the patient experience emotions fully, develop the ability to observe and evaluate the appropriateness of emotions in relation to their life reality, offer alternative interpretations for emotions, such as a sense of capability instead of insecurity, give new meaning to their emotions, and strengthen their ability to choose and shift between strong emotions (Greenberg, 2017). Emotional transformation involves a shared emotional exploration between the therapist and the patient, aimed at helping the patient look inward and identify unconscious emotional patterns, experience emotions in the present, such as sadness or insecurity, and stay with them, address emotional reasons that, from the patient's perspective, lead to substance use, such as protection from feelings of sadness and fear, and express feelings about unmet emotional needs in the past, alongside criticism of significant figures, such as "protective anger" towards figures who neglected them.

Therapeutic Techniques

The "Two Chairs" Technique

The patient sits in one chair and expresses their internal "critical voice," for example: "You are incapable of changing and quitting drugs." In the second chair, the patient presents their "experiencing voice," addressing the pain that originates from self-criticism. The therapist emphasizes hidden strong feelings, such as "protective anger" or a sense of capability, and assists in presenting a new narrative that strengthens the sense of security and ability to cope.

The "Empty Chair" Technique

The patient imagines a significant person and expresses repressed feelings toward them, such as pain, self-criticism, or self-compassion. This technique involves guided imagery, where the addiction-affected patient is asked to "directly address" these figures, present their feelings, and express criticism about the neglect or harm they experienced. For example, they might say to their mother or father, "You ignored me and left me with insecurity and anxiety over the years." The process allows for the creation of a new emotional narrative, where the patient experiences positive emotions of security, control, and capability.

Emotional Pattern Change

The therapist helps reveal painful emotions and link them to new information, for example, a sense of capability alongside fear. The focus is on creating a new emotional pattern where painful emotions like sadness are connected to a sense of strength, allowing for the expression of "protective anger" or criticism.

Psychoeducational Process

The therapist presents the patient with a psychoeducational model that includes an assessment of the emotional difficulties of an addiction-affected patient and identifies emotional, cognitive, and behavioral patterns that contribute to difficulties in emotional regulation. As part of this process, emotional homework assignments are given, designed to deepen the emotional experience and strengthen the ability to cope with emotional issues in ways that promote growth and development. The patient is asked to record their feelings in a feelings journal, and the therapist emphasizes that the patient may experience discomfort, but avoiding emotional experiences may lead to a continued lack of control in their life. The areas of focus in the emotional homework assignments are:

- Strengthening emotional awareness: The addiction-affected patient is asked to dedicate a few minutes each day to reflect on their emotional experiences and describe them in the journal.
- Physical internal focus: The patient is asked to focus on their bodily sensations, identify the emotional words that match these feelings, and record them in the journal.
- Emotional regulation: The therapist guides the patient to take actions for self-soothing in emotionally intense situations, such as deep breathing, calming self-talk, and muscle relaxation. The patient is asked to record in the journal the actions they took and how they affected them.
- Giving new meaning to emotions: In an advanced stage, the addiction-affected patient learns to engage in a cognitive process of transforming maladaptive emotions, such as sadness or tension, into positive emotions of control and confidence. In therapy sessions, the therapist helps the patient process past experiences and connect them to strong emotions.

As part of the conversations, the therapist examines the patient's journal entries together with them—whether there has been improvement in emotional awareness and expression, whether the patient managed to regulate intense emotions, and whether new meaning has been created for their emotions. The documentation and discussion of the homework assignments allow the patient to strengthen emotional awareness, process emotional experiences, create a new narrative based on value, capability, and self-control, and integrate tools for emotional regulation.

Summary: The Power of Emotional Transformation

Processing Unresolved Emotions Toward Attachment Figures

Engaging in emotional transformation deepens the awareness of the addiction-affected patient toward "felt but unclear" experiences. The patient learns to identify emotions such as sadness and insecurity and link them to a sense of anger directed at significant attachment figures. Techniques such as the "empty chair" allow the patient to express unresolved emotions ("unfinished business") like anger, disappointment, and pain toward attachment figures, such as a neglectful parent. A therapy session with Paul illustrates this technique.

Paul, 45, divorced with teenage children, is struggling with illegal gambling addiction. His wife and children severed ties with him three years ago after he accumulated debts and sold family property without their knowledge. Paul reported that he had managed to stop gambling behavior twice, each time for two years, but now lives at his mother's house.

The therapist invites Paul to use the "empty chair" technique and imagine speaking to his mother. Paul expresses anger and frustration that she was not sufficiently involved in his life, saying, "You were always busy with your own issues, and I had to deal with my fears alone."

At the same time, the therapist helps Paul recognize moments of strength from the past, such as his choice to take responsibility for his family during certain periods, strengthening his sense of capability and self-worth.

Processing unresolved emotions through emotional transformation allows the addiction-affected patient, like Paul, to recognize the link between their unresolved emotions and behavior, raise awareness of hidden emotions of value and capability, and build a new emotional narrative that integrates the expression of "protective anger" with a sense of strength and responsibility, enhancing the patient's ability to cope with personal and family challenges on the path to growth and development. The therapist and patient explore events where the patient experienced sadness and shame due to the dismissive behavior of family members, and the therapist helps the patient process those memories while identifying previously hidden positive emotions, such as a sense of value or capability, which emerged when the patient left home and embarked on a new path.

The Critical Voice and the Experiencing Voice

The activation of emotional transformation enables the addiction-affected patient to process memories related to central pain, such as feelings of shame and loneliness resulting from traumatic experiences like neglect or abuse. These emotions often manifest as secondary emotions like anger and offense. The therapist guides the patient to "stay with the pain" and overcome the natural tendency to avoid it, and the patient identifies and brings up strong and repressed feelings of value and capability, integrating them into the emotional memory.

The "two chairs" technique allows the patient to express emotions through the "critical voice" and the "experiencing voice." The critical voice is expressed in statements like, "You are shaming yourself because you can't stop drinking" or "You're too afraid to deal with your father." The therapist then asks the patient to address the self-criticism and also express their strengths and abilities: "I am definitely capable of changing. I managed to stop drinking three times for long periods" or "I have the ability to cope, and I am learning to control myself." This phase focuses on embedding strong emotions of value, self-confidence, and coping ability into the patient's emotional memory. A therapy session with Anthony demonstrates the use of this technique.

Anthony, a 28-year-old single man, struggled with ecstasy abuse for six years. He is currently attending N.A. meetings and has stopped using ecstasy. He reports significant difficulties in his relationship with his parents, especially with his father, making it hard for him to have a conversation without erupting in anger, and describes feelings of loneliness and loss of social connections.

"I hear the sadness that overwhelms you about your failed attempts to connect with family members and others," the therapist says. "These feelings remind you of how your family treated you in the past, especially during your time at boarding school and after the army, and they bring up a lot of anger and loneliness. I want to give you the opportunity to express your emotions. Talk to yourself in the same critical thoughts you hear inside you."

Anthony, somewhat embarrassed, agrees and cooperates. He says, "You really are shaming yourself. How could you not manage to maintain connections with others? You are so insecure that you just gave up on your family connections. You are a coward. You didn't have the courage to face your father, so you just distanced yourself and failed."

"Now, I want you to address the criticism you just expressed," the therapist suggests, "try to also express your strengths."

"Yes," Anthony says, "I am angry and sad about what happened, but I know that I also did a lot of things to change. I managed to stop using ecstasy. I now live in my own apartment, and I'm starting to make new connections in the N.A. group. I realize now that I have strengths. Yes, my father wasn't there for me, but I am learning to believe in myself. I have value, and I am capable of building a better life for myself."

The therapist summarizes, "I want to reinforce what you expressed. You understand the pain you've gone through, but you also recognize your abilities and strengths. You've managed to cope with difficult situations, take control of your life, and begin a significant journey of change. It's not easy, but the strengths you showed will continue to guide you."

The use of the "two chairs" technique allowed Anthony to process his complex emotions, identify his self-criticism, and transform it into an empowering experience voice that reinforced his sense of capability and self-worth. This process emphasizes the importance of embedding strong emotions in the emotional memory as part of creating long-term change.

Acceptance, Compassion, Self-Soothing, and Unmet Needs Expression

Clinical intervention at this stage is designed to help the patient accept themselves while recognizing their abilities and strengths. The addiction-affected patient learns to use meditative activities for self-soothing, helping them cope with maladaptive emotions and create a more balanced emotional experience, characterized by compassion toward themselves for the experiences they missed during the years of substance use. The therapist helps the patient articulate unmet emotional needs, such as a need for safety and protection, and identify how these experiences continue to influence their emotions today. At the same time, the therapist exposes strong and adaptive emotions, such as a sense of pride in the patient's ability to reduce substance use and form new social connections. A therapy session with Thomas illustrates this.

Thomas, a 32-year-old man, has intermittently used ecstasy since he was 18. He describes feelings of anxiety and sadness, struggles with creating interpersonal and romantic relationships, and feels lonely. Thomas lives in his brother's apartment and has minimal contact with his family. He states that ecstasy use helped him forget his pain in the past, but it no longer provides any relief.

" Thomas," the therapist says, "Throughout our sessions, it seems there's a connection between what you're feeling and how your family treated you. You've described moments when you felt humiliated, and they contributed to your sense of worthlessness. I hear your pain and understand how these feelings still affect you today."

"That's true," Thomas sighs, "I feel that my family's disregard for me follows me everywhere. I'm angry at them because they don't give me a chance to change. I don't believe in myself, I am ashamed of myself, and I feel like I have no ability to do anything with my life. Even ecstasy doesn't help me like it did before."

"I hear your self-contempt and your pain. But I want to remind you of something important: We've seen here in our sessions that you've had moments when you demonstrated amazing strengths. For example, your persistence in your studies during the period of estrangement from your mother or your decision to cut ties with friends who led you into substance use. I believe these strengths are still within you, and we can use them for change. What do you think?"

"I understand what you mean. Yes, I managed to persist in my studies despite everything, and that's something I'm proud of. But it doesn't always feel like enough."

"That's definitely something you can be proud of. Let's try to focus more on that. I want us to emphasize the strengths and responsibility you're demonstrating now. I believe you're capable of achieving the change you want. We'll do this together."

As seen in Thomas story, the therapist helped him confront feelings of self-contempt and identify unmet emotional needs, while recognizing and activating hidden strengths from the past. This process helped him shift maladaptive emotions into powerful feelings of value and capability (Timulak et al., 2017).

The recommendation is to conduct six therapy sessions within this stage of emotional transformation.

Emotion-Focused Brief Therapy: Summary and Evaluation

In the summary phase, the therapist and the patient conduct a comprehensive review of the patient's journey within the framework of emotion-focused therapy, including an analysis of the emotional and functional changes the patient has experienced and how these changes have manifested in their overall functioning, family dynamics, employment, and reduction in substance use and addictive behaviors. The therapist and patient review the progress, fluctuations, setbacks, and changes the patient has encountered throughout the stages of treatment. It is crucial to provide reinforcement and evaluation for the achievements and goals reached. During the summary, the therapist emphasizes that the patient is the one who brought about the emotional and behavioral changes themselves, reinforcing feelings of confidence, pride, value, and control, and expressing trust in their ability to maintain these changes in the future. Next, the therapist and patient examine situations that may trigger emotional or functional setbacks in the future, discussing the emotional therapeutic tools acquired and how they can be used independently. Finally, the therapist and patient process feelings like disappointment, anger, and fear toward the conclusion of therapy, emphasizing the use of emotional change language as a tool for dealing with these feelings. The therapist reassures the patient that the "therapeutic door" remains open for them and that they can reach out for advice or support in the future during times of crisis, difficulty, or distress.

It is recommended to hold two dedicated therapy sessions for this stage of summary and evaluation.

7

EMBEDDING ADAPTIVE EMOTION: SELF-EFFICACY

"We cannot experience change, and we cannot progress until we accept who we are. Only then can we experience change, almost without noticing it." (Carl Rogers)

Self-efficacy is one of the central goals of emotion-focused therapy, particularly in individuals dealing with addiction. This sense of efficacy allows patients, who often experience feelings of difficulty, helplessness, and despair, to believe in their ability to change maladaptive patterns, such as excessive substance use, addictive behavior, and inactivity. Embedding self-efficacy focuses on harnessing the necessary forces for significant change in the patient's life, as demonstrated in the session with Mark.

Mark, 35, has been using illicit drugs and marijuana for a decade. Over the years, he has tried to quit through many therapeutic frameworks, but without success, which has contributed to his negative perception of his ability to change his life.

"I don't see any chance," he says to the therapist in despair.

"I actually see something different," the therapist smiles, "I see a high motivation for change: you attend all the sessions regularly, participate actively in the therapy group, are open about your struggles, take responsibility for your past failures in therapy, and are aware of the anxiety that accompanies your day-to-day and significantly hinders you."

It's clear that these words penetrate Mark's heart. He looks at the therapist with hope.

The therapist summarizes, "I am very optimistic about your ability to develop insights, change difficult emotions, and acquire the language of change. I really believe that you are capable."

According to Bandura, self-efficacy is a person's belief in their ability to perform a specific behavior successfully, mobilizing emotional and cognitive resources to create self-motivation for action (Bandura et al., 1999). Self-efficacy develops gradually through cognitive, physiological, social, verbal, and experiential encounters. In the case of someone dealing with addiction, enhancing self-efficacy is the pathway to strengthening their ability to achieve behavioral change and recovery (Shabi, 2024). The patient's involvement in setting therapeutic goals and creating a treatment strategy strengthens their sense of responsibility and decision-making ability (Rathgeber et al., 2019). Additionally, the relationship between the therapist and patient is a driving force in strengthening self-efficacy (Yalom & Leszcz, 2019). The therapist constantly assesses the fit of the treatment to the patient's needs, identifying explicit or implicit pessimistic perceptions that could hinder mobilizing forces for change. According to Miller and Rollnick, self-efficacy is enhanced when patients find a path for change that suits their needs. This sense of self-efficacy allows people to begin a journey of meaningful change (Miller & Rollnick,

2002). The therapeutic encounter with Miriam illustrates this.

Miriam, 29, came to therapy after a referral from her family doctor, who was concerned about the effects of her uncontrolled alcohol consumption. For Miriam, alcohol is more than just a drink—it's what she calls "the engine that keeps me on my feet." She shares that over the years, she has tried to quit drinking, but each attempt left her feeling depressed and sad, ultimately returning her to the same point—the bottle.

Miriam isn't fully committed to the necessity of treatment. "I think I can handle it on my own," she says to her therapist, "I'm not sure this treatment is what I need right now."

The therapist reflects on the reality. "Miriam, I want to share my feelings with you," she says sensitively. "You've told me that you stopped drinking and that you've managed to cope with the urge to drink, but according to the doctor's report and the alcohol tests you've done, you're still drinking at a level that puts you at risk."

Miriam sighs. "Maybe it's just not the right time for me to make a change. I have so much on my mind. Yes, I set myself a goal to stop drinking for at least three weeks, but the truth is, I can't stick to it. I know it's costing me dearly—especially with my family—but this is who I am. What can I really do?"

The therapist listens to her with genuine interest and says, "I hear you, Miriam, and I see that you see things differently. You feel like you can't handle it, and I can feel your fear of change—maybe the fear that if you fail to stop, you'll experience self-disappointment. But I also see something else—I see that you care deeply about yourself, even though you feel stuck. I also see that you're capable of more than you believe right now."

The therapist pauses for a few moments to let the message sink in and adds, "I want to remind you of some important things. Your mother said, and you've shared, that you've stopped drinking on your own in the past, and for a significant period. During that time, you managed to integrate into your work, improve your relationships with your family, and achieve goals that matter to you. This shows that you have strength. I'm here to help you find additional ways that can help you cope. I believe in you, Miriam."

The conversation between the therapist and Miriam illustrates the significant differences between patients in terms of motivation for change and the ability to mobilize emotional and cognitive resources to deal with personal challenges. This factor depends on the characteristics of the emotional and behavioral difficulty, as well as the positive or negative experiences the person struggling with addiction has had in the past, and whether or not there is family support. Strengthening self-efficacy in a marginalized population, such as those affected by addiction, requires providing unwavering support to the patient. The therapist must help the patient identify hidden and visible strengths that have allowed them to experience successes in the past, as well as supportive resources, such as family and social connections, which may serve as sources of help in the therapeutic journey

(Wiebe & Johnson, 2016). Additionally, strengthening the patient's ability to make decisions about their life independently is a central process in emotion-focused therapy. The therapist can advise the patient on various issues they are grappling with and present alternative solutions for problems in the area of addiction, as long as the advice is based on mutual exploration and inquiry, ultimately leaving the patient to choose the solution that best meets their needs. A process in which the therapist makes decisions for the patient, without dialogue or considering alternatives, may harm the patient's sense of self-efficacy, leave them passive, and prevent them from experiencing a sense of self-actualization and independence (Goldman & Rousmaniere, 2021). The therapist must remember that the knowledge they have is partial and subjective in relation to the dilemmas the patient faces. In other words, advice does not harm the patient's self-efficacy; on the contrary, it serves as model for ways in which informed decisions can be made, with care, attention, and concern from the therapist. Advice can reduce the emotional isolation that patients often feel in their daily lives (Hohman, 2012). The conversation with Jason in the therapeutic session illustrates this.

Jason, a 22-year-old young man, has been using cannabis problematically for six years. Despite the treatment center being close to his home, he rarely attends meetings. He was referred to therapy by his family doctor, who expressed great concern about his health and mental condition.

In the first meetings, Jason appeared withdrawn and

barely spoke. It seemed that the pressure his family placed on him regarding cannabis use was affecting him greatly, but he didn't know how to cope with it.

Jason arrives at the current session with a request. "I hope I can get some advice here and a clear explanation on how to stop using cannabis," he says honestly. "My whole family is stressed because I keep using it. I'll do whatever you tell me."

The therapist follows his words and shares her thoughts with him. "In the last session, you brought up the request for me to guide you and tell you what to do. I feel it will be difficult to achieve real change if the action to stop using cannabis doesn't come from you. I also see that you're under a lot of pressure from the thought of living without cannabis. You mentioned that the last time you tried to stop, you felt anxiety and depression. I feel your struggle and the lack of confidence you're describing – this is very natural in this situation."

Jason shrugs. "What you're saying is very true," he admits, "but I understood from friends who were here at the center that the whole idea of therapy is for them to guide me, to tell me what to do. I just can't manage on my own."

"The idea of therapy is indeed to help you," the therapist explains. "Among other things, by addressing emotions like the insecurity you've started to talk about and the shame you feel toward your family because of your substance use. We will try to understand together why you've been experiencing a lack of control over your life for the past few years. I am here to assist you. I will help you with information and by considering various options for change, but ultimately, you are the one who has to decide what is the right path for you. I see that you have the strengths and abilities to deal with this. Believe in yourself."

The approach of positive psychology is another effective framework for promoting self-efficacy among those affected by addiction. This approach focuses on embedding positive reinforcements and strategies aimed at evoking positive emotions, optimism, and happiness, alongside learning adaptive interpersonal strategies (Bolier et al., 2013; Sheldon & Lyubomirsky, 2006). There are several ways to promote self-efficacy in the spirit of positive psychology:

- The patient is invited to send feedback or a written message to close individuals, expressing gratitude for positive experiences they have had in their relationship with them (Sheldon & Lyubomirsky, 2006).
- The therapist helps the patient struggling with addiction to broaden their awareness of positive traits they possess, such as humanity, creativity, and kindness (Peterson & Seligman, 2004).
- The therapist focuses on the positive aspects of the patient's life and highlights their hidden and visible strengths, which may contribute to positive adaptation and an optimistic outlook for the future (Peterson et al., 2012).
- The therapist directs the addiction-affected patient to engage in volunteer work, with the aim of experiencing positive emotions, a sense of

pride, and a positive self-image based on contributing to others (Pressman et al., 2015).

Processes for promoting self-efficacy and positive personal reinforcement within an emotion-focused interpersonal therapy framework are demonstrated in the therapeutic conversation with Mori.

Mori, a 33-year-old single man, returned to using heroin after a four-year period in which he was treated with methadone replacement therapy. The first meeting with the therapist at the psychosocial center, which Mori attends independently, reveals a frustrated, tired, and deeply sorrowful person. He speaks openly about the sense of failure that accompanies his return to substance use and describes a difficult childhood marked by violence from his father and a lack of attention to his needs from other family members. "Most of the time, I'm at home, in a shared apartment, but I hardly talk to them," he says. "I worked intermittently in moving, but it didn't give me any meaning." The therapist observes that his sense of self-efficacy is very low, and he has almost no expectations for the future.

"I hear the distress you're describing," she says gently. "Your history, the violence you experienced, and the lack of attention to your needs – all of these are heavy burdens that follow you everywhere. I sense that the trauma you've endured has left you feeling hopeless, with a lack of trust in yourself and in others. Perhaps returning to heroin use is a way to avoid dealing with the deep pain that surrounds you. Am I right?"

"You might be surprised," Mori says quietly, "but to be honest, I pretty much agree with what my family thinks about me. I've tried to change several times, but maybe I'm just not good enough. I can't meet the goals I set for myself. Maybe this is just my situation."

The therapist nods empathetically and says, "I have to say, I see things differently, Mori. You come here consistently, you make efforts to be honest about what you're going through now and what happened in the past. You talk about your pains and the sense of rejection that accompanies you. You defined drugs as something that alleviates your anxiety, but you also saw that they caused you many complications – with the law, and with your health. I actually see an initial willingness for change. You made the independent decision in the past to join a drug replacement program, prevented your friends from dropping out of it, and you're volunteering here at the center for various tasks. All of this shows that you have strengths and that you can succeed."

In conclusion, strengthening self-efficacy among patients dealing with addiction within an emotion-focused therapy framework is based on providing tools and coping skills for complex problems, while reinforcing the individual's confidence in their ability to face challenges. The therapist strengthens the patient's involvement in the therapeutic process, including setting the strategy, goals, and treatment plan, with the aim of encouraging a sense of personal responsibility and active collaboration. The therapist encourages the addiction-affected patient to take initiative and experiment with new ways of dealing with their difficulties, with the goal of increasing their sense of self-efficacy. They provide consistent, unconditional emotional support while identifying and reinforcing the patient's internal resources, which they may be unaware of. Additionally, the therapist encourages the patient's independence in areas such as planning, decision-making, and problem-solving, with tailored guidance (Hohman, 2012). A sense of self-efficacy is an essential anchor in the recovery process, allowing the addiction-affected patient to achieve significant progress, adapt to changes, and feel confident in their ability to control their life.

8

EMOTION-FOCUSED THERAPY AND HARM REDUCTION

"To dismiss addictions as bad habits or self-destructive behavior is an easy way to ignore their functionality in the lives of addicts." (Vincent Felitti)

The harm reduction approach aims to reduce the negative impacts associated with addictive behavior, including the misuse of drugs and alcohol. The approach focuses on providing various therapeutic interventions, including:

• Pharmacological Treatment: Administering medications to alleviate addiction symptoms and reduce the bodily harm caused by substance use.

• Medical Interventions: Treating medical conditions that arise from the use of psychoactive substances.

• Psychosocial Support: Emotional and social support aimed at assisting in both personal and community aspects.

The primary goal of harm reduction is to alleviate mental, emotional, and physical symptoms for patients who continue to use psychoactive substances while improving their quality of life and reducing the harms associated with addiction (Fox et al., 2013; Lev-Ran et al., 2014; Johnson, 2020).

Ronald, 38 years old, has been struggling with heroin use

for fifteen years. About three years ago, he was diagnosed with antisocial personality disorder in the mental health system. Ronald served a two-year prison sentence for assault, and according to him, his time in prison left him feeling alienated and frustrated with the world.

The doctors who treated him recommended long-term pharmacological treatment that could ease his struggle with long-term addiction. However, Ronald rejected this option outright. "Either I manage to stay completely clean of drugs, or I continue using," he said firmly.

Ronald expressed a negative stance towards the entire treatment system. He had difficulty believing that treatment could provide him with a real solution to his needs or change his situation. In the psychosocial addiction sessions, he attended, Ronald rarely spoke about himself.

The therapist noticed his self-doubts and the despair accompanying him, and now attempts to approach him with an accepting, tailored approach, offering to explore together different ways that could help him overcome his mistrust—both in himself and in the personal change process.

"I'm here for you," she says gently, "I believe you can find another way to deal with the difficulties you're describing."

However, Ronald finds it hard to cooperate. He keeps emotional distance and avoids committing to the process. After a short period, he decides to leave the treatment framework.

In light of Ronald's story, one could evaluate that presenting an alternative treatment option, such as a combined intervention of the harm reduction approach (Johnson, 2020) and emotion-focused therapy (Greenberg, 2017), could have provided a response to his dilemmas and increased his willingness to give treatment a chance. Populations on the addiction spectrum, particularly those dealing with comorbidities, are often characterized by avoidance of listening to emotions, overwhelming emotions that they are unable to control, trauma, mental difficulties, and health conditions. The intensive use of psychoactive substances serves many as a "medicine" to numb emotional and physical pain. However, it fails to break the cycle of distress and despair (Shabi, 2024).

Human Needs at the Center

Like emotion-focused therapy, the harm reduction approach draws inspiration from humanistic psychology (Rogers, 1957), which places human needs at the center and views interpersonal therapeutic relationships, as well as medical, psychological, and social assistance, as the way to promote the mental health of the patient. The approach accepts the assumption that some individuals in the population will struggle to accept assistance within a framework that aims for complete abstinence from substances (Mata, 2021). It provides medical and psychosocial pathways aimed at reducing harm, improving the health of addiction sufferers, strengthening their proactivity, and promoting better adaptation to reality (Wamel et al., 2021), as seen in the story of Kenneth.

Kenneth, 48 years old, has been struggling with alcohol addiction for fifteen years. Over the years, he has tried various treatments but found himself repeatedly drawn back into his old habits. In the past two years, in addition to his addiction, he has been suffering from untreated depression that burdens him even more. He has often promised himself and his family that he would stop his uncontrollable drinking, but apart from brief periods of success, he struggled to keep his promises. Now, having been unemployed for a year and a half, Kenneth feels lost, disconnected, and full of shame.

The therapist gently but decisively approaches him: "Given the current situation, after all the attempts you've made to quit, perhaps it's time to consider a different approach. What do you think about setting a new goal—gradually reducing the amount of alcohol you drink, rather than complete cessation? This might be a more effective and appropriate step for you. Does this option seem possible to you?"

Kenneth sighs. "This thought has crossed my mind here and there," he says quietly, "but I have no confidence in my ability to achieve anything related to alcohol. After so many years and so many failures—I've lost count of how many times I tried to quit. There are things that just don't change in me. And now, once again, I promised my family that that's it, I'm done with it. I'm ashamed of myself."

The therapist offers another perspective: "I hear the suffering you're going through and the difficulty from the failures you've experienced so far. But it's important to remember that you've made efforts—and in some cases, you succeeded, even for certain periods. Today, you're consistently participating in individual and group therapy, you're involved and sharing what you're going through. That's not insignificant. I sense your desire for change, but also the fear that this current attempt won't succeed. You're giving a lot of space to the part of you that is afraid and failing and silencing the part of you that has strengths and capabilities.

What do you think about trying emotion-focused therapy? It's a treatment that can help you deal with the depression you've been feeling so intensely over the past year, process those emotions, and receive tailored mental support. At the same time, we can work on a plan to reduce alcohol consumption—not complete cessation, but small, tailored steps that will make it easier for you. I believe you can make a change in your life."

The intervention plan proposed for Kenneth is based on the assumption that, at this point in time, Kenneth is unable to fully stop his addictive behavior. Therefore, the therapeutic approach combining harm reduction focuses on building a personal and supportive therapeutic framework that focuses on emotional processes such as awareness of non-adaptive emotions, emotional regulation, and transformation into feelings of control and capability, controlled reduction of substance use, and medical consultation. In the case of opioid addicts, long-term pharmacological treatment with methadone or buprenorphine is provided, which can contribute to functional recovery (Fox et al., 2013). The harm reduction approach includes a wide range of medical and psychosocial responses, including participation in a needle exchange program aimed at reducing transmission of diseases such as Hepatitis C and HIV; provision of naloxone, which prevents death from opioid overdose; and long-term pharmacological treatment, such as methadone or buprenorphine, to reduce cravings for heroin use. In some countries, harm reduction programs also include the injection of heroin that the patient brings to the clinic or even the provision of clean heroin supplied by the state (Najavits et al., 2005).

The harm reduction approach presents many challenges for patients suffering from addiction, as can be seen in an excerpt from a therapeutic conversation with John:

John, 42 years old, married with two children, has been struggling with heroin addiction for thirteen years. In the last three years, he participated in a long-term pharmacological treatment program using Suboxone, which was a bright spot in his long and difficult journey. However, after it was discovered that he had resumed using street drugs, it was decided to discontinue his participation in the program.

In a conversation with the therapist at the psychosocial center, John appears agitated and withdrawn, dealing with feelings of shame, disappointment, and anger.

The therapist carefully opens the conversation: "I hear your frustration and disappointment about the decision to stop your participation in the program. It seems that you feel that the staff at the drug treatment center gave up on you as if they didn't care about you. This reminds me of what you shared in the past about your father's behavior, where he said he didn't trust you and didn't believe you could stick to your goals. I guess this is part of what's fueling your anger now. Am I on the right track?"

John nods sadly. "Yes, you're absolutely right," he says in a choked voice. "But I have to admit, it's not just them – I have responsibility for what happened. In the end, I broke the rules. I had another crisis with my wife, and I was frustrated. I felt like I had no way to cope, so I turned to what I knew – I used. I thought it would calm me down, but it just made the situation worse."

He pauses for a moment, his eyes wet. "Still, the staff could have met me halfway, tried to understand me," he says. "This really reminds me of my parents. I was a child who just wanted someone to believe in me, and I never got that. Now I feel the same way again."

For several moments, a heavy silence fills the room. The therapist looks at John and says, "I hear the shame you carry with you, just as you described the feelings you had at home with your parents. It's clear that the recent crisis with your wife and the staff's response deepened the wound. But John, I also see the progress you've made. In the past three years, you've shown yourself and others that you are capable of change. You joined a long-term pharmacological treatment program, stopped using heroin for an extended period, and succeeded in maintaining a job at a food store. You've come a long way."

"The choice now is in your hands. You have the opportunity to fix things. I believe in you and your ability to cope with this crisis. Maybe we can think together about returning to the treatment program, this time with a clear goal of processing the recent crisis with your wife and working through the feelings of pain and anger related to your memories from home. What do you think? Would you like to try again? I will be here with you all the way."

Interpersonal therapy integrated into a harm reduction program does not require the patient to completely stop substance use in order to receive treatment. Its main goal is to improve the quality of life for individuals affected by addiction (Najavits, 2002). This approach encourages reinforcing efforts for change, even if they involve small and initial steps. Setting measurable goals for acquiring a language of change in the context of addiction may reduce patients' fears of failure and the feeling of stagnation (Miller & Rollnick, 2013). Numerous studies show that focused treatment for those affected by addiction, which includes emotional, behavioral, medical responses, and problem-solving, is an effective action that leads to gradual positive change (Najavits et al., 2005). Mata (2021) found that combining psychosocial and medical treatment significantly reduces street drug use, decreases overdose death rates, improves social and family functioning, and even reduces criminal involvement. The positive impact of a harm reduction program increases when, in addition to psychosocial and medical treatment, solutions in the areas of housing and employment are provided. However, before deciding on the patient's integration into the program, the mutual interests of the patient and the therapist must be assessed, potential risks to the patient and their environment must be identified, and clear standards and action plans must be defined for the implementation of the program (White & Popovits, 2001).

Harm Reduction: Dilemmas and Challenges

However, the implementation of the harm reduction approach raises significant ethical questions:

- Does long-term pharmacological treatment or the provision of drugs under controlled conditions actually reduce street drug use and the associated risks?
- What is the state's responsibility towards patients participating in programs that provide drugs?
- What is the degree of responsibility of doctors in providing drugs through the state to patients who inject them themselves?

The answers to these questions suggest that harm reduction programs, alongside reducing the risk of street drug use and lowering the mortality rate (Mata, 2021), place significant responsibility on the state to provide continuous support and guidance to participants. This presents a challenge for policymakers and therapists, who are required to strike a balance between implementing the program and reducing risk among its participants, while also providing a comprehensive and inclusive response to their needs.

In conclusion, the emotion-focused approach and the harm reduction approach, inspired by humanistic psychology, place the individual's needs at the center.

Their goal is to reduce risks, lower mortality, and improve the quality of life for individuals affected by addiction. The integration of these approaches in the treatment of populations struggling to stop substance use includes providing pharmacological, medical, and supportive responses, alongside encouraging emotional expression, emotional regulation, reflection, and emotional transformation (Greenberg, 2017). The implementation of this integrated approach emphasizes the patient's freedom of choice, without imposing rigid conditions regarding substance use. The patient can choose between reducing use, continuing use under supervision, or complete abstinence (Mata, 2021). The belief is that this program, which combines emotional change and harm reduction, will allow the patient to reduce risks, strengthen their self-efficacy, and fulfill their personal potential.

> "Finding your own way up the mountain gives a sense of strength much greater and more meaningful than walking the familiar path." (Karen Horney)

9

FACING THE FUTURE

ADDICTION EMOTION-FOCUSED THERAPY IN THE DIGITAL SPACE

Edward, a 27-year-old man working in the IT field, has been using stimulants since his release from the army. In a conversation with his therapist at an addiction treatment center, he expresses feelings of shame and self-anger for not being able to stop using substances. "I feel like it's only making my anxiety and depression worse," he says, "and it's affecting my ability to function at work, which is the most important thing to me right now."

During the initial intake sessions, or appears lost and frustrated. On one hand, he expresses disappointment that he hasn't been able to progress and achieve his goals, such as strengthening his skills as a programmer and building an independent professional career. On the other hand, he expresses frustration that he can't stop using drugs and that, according to him, he is "in the same place as real addicts."

When the therapist suggests he participate in an assessment group at the center or strongly refuses. "No way I'm coming to sit there," he says, "I can't handle staying in a place like that." Instead, he asks if there's a way to get help without coming to the treatment center.

The therapist hesitates for a moment and then cautiously asks, "What do you think about the possibility of having online meetings in a digital space? This process would include an assessment and short-term counseling, which could happen at times that are convenient for both of us. We can start with a basic introduction, talk about the substances you use, understand how they affect you, and explore treatment directions."

Edward appears hesitant. "I don't understand how this could work. How can you treat something so complex without being physically present?"

The therapist smiles encouragingly. "For me too, this is a new approach, but I see it as an opportunity to try something different. It allows you to receive help without having to deal with the difficulty of physically coming to the center. We can work together to overcome the resistance and build a process that fits you."

In the wake of the COVID-19 pandemic, crisis situations, and ongoing military events that limited the possibility of face-to-face treatments, the use of digital treatments expanded significantly. The central role of the internet in everyday life, including among people dealing with addiction, created an opportunity to implement emotion-focused discourse in this space. This discourse integrates the key principles of emotion-focused interpersonal therapy: acquiring emotional awareness, emotional expression, emotional regulation, and emotional transformation (McGuinty et al., 2016).

Emotion-focused therapy in the digital space is implemented through a variety of platforms and technologies, such as web-based systems, apps, computer software, video calls, Zoom, Google Meet, and phone calls. Geller and other researchers note that digital therapy, which can sometimes simulate face-to-face therapy, offers significant advantages in promoting treatment availability, flexible scheduling, and the accessibility of information for treated populations (Geller, 2020; Weinberg & Rolnick, 2019). The advantages of this therapy are particularly prominent in populations that experience feelings of stigma, exclusion, limitation, or illness, and who sometimes avoid or struggle to attend face-to-face treatment. The digital space offers access to treatment and even the first opportunity to receive help. Moreover, it bridges geographic distances between the patient and the therapist, saves time, and even expands treatment to include systemic interventions, such as family involvement (Agar, 2019; Kocsii & Yellowlees, 2018).

Online Presence and Interpersonal Connection

Emotional therapy in the digital space requires creating a space that allows for true therapeutic presence, interpersonal connection, and the building of a therapeutic alliance using unconditional support language, empathy, and acceptance (Brubcher & Wiebe, 2019; Greenman & Johnson, 2013). In collaboration with the patient, the therapist defines the interpersonal therapy goals and the means to achieve them. The therapeutic dialogue involves processing the verbal and non-verbal expressions of a patient suffering from addiction, along with monitoring the connections between physical communication and verbal activity and their meanings. The therapist is required to be deeply involved and proactive, focusing on identifying physical signs that indicate avoidance of emotional listening, denial, or difficulty bringing emotions to awareness. The therapist's role includes interpreting these signs, providing emotional reflection, and assisting in building insights into maladaptive emotional patterns, such as despair or anger (Greenberg, 2015). When the patient struggles to express emotions, the therapist revisits unprocessed parts of the emotional dialogue to help them build a new narrative of their emotional experience, one based on feelings of capability and control (Brubcher & Wiebe, 2019). Additionally, a therapist working with addiction patients in the digital space needs technological proficiency (Agosta, 2020) and familiarity with the potential difficulties the patient may have in connecting to and using the digital system. The therapist should prepare the patient for the online therapy process and offer early solutions for any technological issues that could cause stress or pressure. Awareness of factors in the patient's environment that could interfere with the therapeutic discourse is critical (Weinberg & Rolnick, 2019) in the context of online therapy. A patient at home may fear expressing their emotions if they think someone from their family is listening in (Simpson et al., 2021). In such cases, the therapist must explore with the patient the possibility of moving to an alternative space where they can feel safe and reduce distractions.

EFT for Addiction Patients in the Digital Space: Stages

1. Initial Introduction and Assessment: At the beginning of the process, the therapist conducts an initial face-to-face conversation with the patient to assess the personal background, reasons

for seeking treatment, the nature of the difficulty, and the ability to establish interpersonal connections within the digital framework. This assessment provides the foundation for understanding the needs and possibilities for treatment.

2. Information Accessibility: The therapist provides the patient with verbal and written information about the field of addiction, characteristics of addiction problems, types of psychoactive substances, and behavioral addictions. The therapist also explains the principles of emotion-focused interpersonal therapy, including its application in the digital space. At this stage, the patient must give consent to participate in the process.
3. Initial Diagnosis: The therapist conducts a conversation with the patient for the purpose of creating an interpersonal connection and conducting an initial assessment of the addiction situation using digital diagnostic questionnaires, such as the ASSIST or ASI.
4. Joint Creation of a Therapeutic Plan: The therapist and the patient, who is struggling with addiction, collaboratively define an emotion-focused treatment plan tailored to the patient's individual needs. This plan is sent to the patient in a digital format.
5. Short-Term Emotion-Focused Therapy: The therapy is conducted via video, with an emphasis on building interpersonal relationships,

deepening the patient's awareness of maladaptive emotions, and emotional regulation, and transforming them into positive emotions such as control and self-worth (McGuinty et al., 2016; Greenberg, 2017).

6. Addressing Non-Verbal Communication and Behavioral Patterns: In therapy, the therapist attends to bodily expressions such as facial expressions and physical symptoms of the patient struggling with addiction (Cassidy & Shaver, 2016). These signs may indicate sadness, anger, or defense mechanisms aimed at avoiding disturbing emotional content from the past (Brubcher & Wiebe, 2019). The therapist also observes behavioral patterns during the conversation, such as interrupting the dialogue, using a phone, or distancing from the screen, and explores their meaning. This may stem from resistance to the process, dissatisfaction, or difficulty with emotional reflection (Johnson, 2019).
7. Regulating Intense Emotions: In emotionally overwhelming situations, the therapist employs emotion-focused techniques that are also used in face-to-face therapy, such as mindfulness and guided imagery (Dunn et al., 2013). These techniques help the patient focus non-judgmentally on their emotional experiences and regulate intense emotions.

Challenges and Opportunities in Digital Therapy for Individuals Coping with Addiction

The challenges in emotion-focused therapy in the digital space for Individuals Coping with Addiction are similar to those in face-to-face therapy, including resistance to the process, difficulty with emotional expression, and emotion regulation. However, the digital platform offers opportunities for greater flexibility, making therapy accessible to patients who struggle to attend in person, and strengthening the availability of therapeutic support even in emergency situations. A therapy session with Linda illustrates the advantages of digital therapy.

Linda, a twenty-five-year-old, has been struggling with opioid prescription drug addiction for three years. During her first session with the therapist at an addiction treatment center, she openly shared that she had managed to stop her intensive use of drugs for five months, but recently relapsed. She stated that she obtains the drugs both through her doctors and other means.

"I haven't been feeling well lately," Linda admits. "I'm constantly anxious, feeling sadness I don't know where it's coming from. The medication doesn't help me like it used to."

When the therapist asks about her intentions to continue therapy, Linda responds firmly, "I don't intend to come back here. Neither the people nor this place are right for me. I don't have any connection with the people here, and I don't have their problems. It's just not for me."

The therapist tries to clarify that this is personal therapy with no interaction with other patients, but Linda is resolute. "I don't want to expose myself to other people," she says. "I don't think therapy is what I need right now."

The therapist suggests an alternative: online therapy. Initially, Linda responds with hesitation, but after a few days, she reaches out and says she is willing to try.

The first online session is emotionally distant. Linda appears remote, mostly speaking about general topics, and is reluctant to address her personal difficulties. "I still don't understand how this medium is supposed to work," she says.

The therapist smiles encouragingly. "It's not that different from what you already know – talking on Zoom, texting on WhatsApp. So far, there haven't been any technical issues, so I think there's something else getting in the way. I hear that you're not feeling comfortable, and I want to understand why. What are you experiencing right now?"

Linda takes a deep breath. "The truth is, I'm confused,' she replies. "It's not just the Zoom call, it's something deeper. I thought these talks would clarify my relationship with the drugs – why I need them so much and why I can't stop. Every time, I go back to that 'Zaldiar.' On the one hand, it helps me, but on the other hand, it's destroying me."

The therapist nods. "It's important to me that you tell me if something is unclear to you at any point. I want us to overcome the physical distance and find an emotional connection. I hear that you're starting to honestly address what you're going through. It seems like you don't want to face these difficulties alone. Even if this is happening remotely, there's an opportunity to explore what you're feeling, understand what drives you, and work on changing the emotions that cause you suffering. Am I right?"

Geller (2020) notes that the central challenge in emotion-focused therapy in the digital space is creating a therapeutic experience that is as close as possible to face-to-face therapy. To address this challenge, the therapist must ensure a digital space that is empathetic and inclusive, allowing for continuous verbal interpersonal sharing, emotional therapeutic presence, and open feedback. This space must enable the patient to express emotions, regulate them, and gain insights into their maladaptive emotions (Geller, 2017, 2019; Greenberg, 2015). In cases where emotional interpersonal processes in the digital space do not succeed in fulfilling the therapy stages and clinical tasks of emotion-focused therapy, it may be necessary to consider transitioning to face-to-face therapy. In such cases, in-person therapy will allow for emotional and behavioral change, which will be reflected in reduced dependence on psychoactive substances (McGuinty et al., 2016; Pugh et al., 2020; Shabi, 2021).

Summary: Conditions for Optimal Online Addiction Treatment

Emotion-focused therapy for individuals affected by addiction and at-risk populations can also be implemented in the digital space, provided the following conditions are met:

- Technical Control: Both the therapist and the

patient must have full control over the digital system.

- Availability and Flexibility: The therapist's availability, scheduling flexibility based on the patient's needs, and adapting the therapeutic setting.
- Building Interpersonal Connection: The therapist should foster relationships of sharing, support, containment, and empathy.
- Implementing Core Therapy Components: Enhancing the patient's awareness of their emotions, emotional regulation, and emotional transformation where negative emotions like anxiety, loneliness, and insecurity are transformed into positive emotions of capability, control, and pride.

Integrating these components can help the patient acquire the language of behavioral change, which includes a process for reducing or stopping the use of psychoactive substances and improving personal functioning.

10

EFT WITH INDIVIDUALS DEALING WITH ADDICTION: CHALLENGES AND SOLUTIONS

Treatment for individuals dealing with addiction presents challenges, including difficulties in establishing interpersonal connections, building a therapeutic alliance, and managing chronic, painful emotions characteristic of patients who do not believe in themselves or the therapeutic system

Intense Emotions

Patients on the addiction continuum often experience intense emotions of anger and frustration originating from past traumas, including feelings of humiliation due to injuries or social barriers. The use of psychoactive substances serves as a kind of "temporary healing process" for them, thus distancing them from treatment aimed at personal change and altering patterns of substance use. The response to these difficulties focuses on the patient's emotional experiences and their transformation. Interpersonal therapy focuses on strengthening the patient's awareness of their emotions, providing opportunities to express those emotions, and enhancing self-efficacy and strength can improve the patient's willingness to engage in and persist with the therapeutic process. The therapist works to strengthen the patient's sense of safety through the language of empathy and unconditional support. This approach allows for inclusion, understanding, and identification with the patient's experiences of loss and deprivation, creating a corrective emotional experience and providing a secure foundation. This process strengthens the patient's self-efficacy and encourages them to believe in their ability to change. The therapy also includes techniques for physical and emotional relaxation, such as meditation and guided imagery, aimed at directing the patient's attention non-judgmentally to their physical and emotional experiences. Greenberg and Goldman (2008) emphasize the importance of addressing unmet needs, such as emotional deprivation or neglect, and performing actions to transform intense emotions into those aligned with reality.

Resistance

Patients dealing with addiction may express resistance to treatment both openly and covertly. Sometimes they try to focus on facts and avoid articulating their emotional struggles clearly (Greenberg, 2015). The therapist will attempt to "move" maladaptive emotions, such as insecurity, tension, anger, frustration, or fear, explain the background of their formation, and assist the patient in replacing them with positive emotions, such as control, pride, and confidence. This process strengthens the patient's sense of efficacy and their ability to reflect on the progress they've made and enact change.

Everyday Barriers

The treatment requires a combination of emotional interventions and practical interventions that impact the patients with addiction in everyday life. This integration allows for addressing daily barriers such as lack of employment, housing difficulties, issues in relationships with family members, and challenges with the law (Aharonovich et al., 2018). Practical interventions include rights advocacy, personal guidance, job placement, and advocacy. These actions can reduce stress and allow the patient to emotionally disengage and participate in therapy. However, it is important to examine with the patient whether focusing on practical issues serves as a mechanism for avoiding dealing with emotional pain (Elliot, 2004). The therapist and patient need to process this issue and explore ways to address both emotional difficulties and practical challenges simultaneously.

Difficulty Identifying Core Pain

Some patients struggle to define their central emotional difficulties and present a clear narrative of their emotions (Timulak, 2015). The therapist needs to identify emotional patterns and assist the patient in processing the core pain they are experiencing. The therapy focuses on identifying maladaptive emotional experiences, understanding their impact on their lives, and identifying adaptive emotional alternatives, such as control and self-confidence. Patients affected by addiction who have difficulty expressing their core pain may struggle to achieve emotional transformation. At this stage, the focus should be on processing traumatic events and validating their unmet needs, such as a lack of protection or long-term support. This includes processing traumatic events and expressing emotions such as pain or shame, using "protective anger" in a way that allows emotional release and critical expression toward significant figures responsible for the traumatic experiences, and encouraging the patient to experience compassion and empathy for themselves and recognize their self-worth.

Self-Criticism

Patients on the addiction continuum who tend to self-criticize or feel self-contempt may struggle with reflective processes (Timulak & McElvaney, 2018). In these cases, the therapist will use empathetic language and support to help the patient accept themselves and recognize their strengths. Therapy includes emotional reflection, role-playing, and tasks that evoke emotions, focusing on creating a new narrative based on a positive self-image and a sense of efficacy.

In summary, the emotion-focused interpersonal approach with patients dealing with addiction involves challenges such as difficulty in forming interpersonal connections, managing emotions, and a tendency toward rationalization. The therapy focuses on helping the patient construct a new narrative of their emotional experiences, with an emphasis on embedding strong, adaptive emotions, processing maladaptive emotions, and strengthening proactivity and adaptability. In this way, the patient becomes an active partner in the change process.

> "Most people see what is, and never see what can be."
> (Albert Einstein)

SUMMARY AND REFLECTIONS

"At any given moment, we have two choices: to move forward toward growth or to move backward and remain where we are" (Maslow)

This book focuses on individuals dealing with significant emotional difficulties, including trauma and anxiety, which often lead to a vicious cycle of addiction to psychoactive substances and addictive behaviors. These vulnerable individuals tend to have difficulty expressing emotions, lack awareness of their feelings, and struggle to manage intense emotions. For them, the solution to their emotional and behavioral challenges, which are sometimes described as unbearable, is the excessive use of psychoactive substances. However, this solution is only temporary, as it does not resolve the underlying issue but creates a new problem, addiction to substances and addictive behaviors, that worsens the emotional and behavioral state.

The book presents an approach that offers a solution for populations struggling with emotional and behavioral challenges, through therapy that focuses on changing emotions as a basis for behavioral change. EFT emphasizes creating strong positive emotions, such as self-efficacy and control. Numerous studies, including the current one, indicate that strengthening these feelings may motivate patients to initiate change and improve their functioning. The emotion-focused approach emphasizes the need to bring the patient in touch with their emotional pain, which is often the result of traumatic experiences. The goal of therapy is to promote the change of maladaptive emotions and replace them with more adaptive emotions, allowing for better emotional functioning. Populations struggling with addiction often experience intense emotional pain, arising from humiliation, rejection, and personal isolation. The therapeutic process involves exposing and understanding these pains, with the aim of providing the patient with a sense of strength and self-efficacy. The proposed therapy in this approach focuses on correcting the patient's emotional mechanism by replacing maladaptive defensive emotions, such as sadness from prolonged emotional injury, with adaptive emotions like optimism and belief in the ability to achieve emotional well-being. This approach aims to help the patient disengage from excessive use of psychoactive substances or reduce it while achieving emotional balance and strengthening the sense of control over their life. The therapeutic process described in this book focuses on enhancing the patient's ability to identify and accumulate new information about positive emotions that have previously been hidden, and changing negative memories related to feelings of rejection and helplessness (Greenberg, 2015; Shabi, 2024). As research shows, Emotion-Focused Therapy contributes to emotional relief and positive changes in populations experiencing trauma, anxiety, and depression (Eliott et al., 2018; Angus et al., 2015). The book suggests that populations struggling with addiction could also benefit significantly from this unique therapeutic approach (Shabi, 2024). One of the key components of this approach is emotional transformation

(Greenberg, 2017), which aims to replace maladaptive emotions, like anxiety, with stronger and more adaptive emotions such as self-efficacy and self-control (Timulak & Mcelvaney, 2018). This process allows patients to process their emotions, integrate new feelings into their emotional system, and create a new positive narrative for their emotional experiences (Greenberg, 2017).

A study conducted with a population dealing with addiction, who were staying in seven therapeutic communities, examined the effects of emotional therapy combined with complementary psychosocial intervention. The study found that patients were able to regulate intense emotions such as rage and anger to a level that allowed for effective emotional processing. This process included transforming feelings of shame and despair into feelings of self-control and confidence, which in turn contributed to significant emotional change. This emotional change also led to behavioral change, manifested in sustained participation in therapeutic programs, successful life adaptation, and abstinence from drugs and alcohol (Shabi, 2024).

The current book contributes uniquely to the research literature on Emotion-Focused Therapy for populations struggling with addiction in two main aspects:

1. Enhancing Emotional Mapping Ability: Emotion-Focused Therapy offers tools that strengthen patients' awareness of the emotional addiction continuum, often underlying the acute distress they experience. This process includes identifying emotions like fear, anger, and sadness, along with

a deep understanding of the factors that led to their creation, such as experiences of abuse or humiliation.

2. Emotion Flexibility and Regulation: Addiction patients learn to cope with maladaptive emotions through a new perspective that allows for alternative interpretations of their feelings. For example, feelings of helplessness can be replaced by a sense of control, and despair can turn into confidence. This process emphasizes the connection between emotion, thought, and behavioral change, ultimately enabling the reduction or cessation of psychoactive substance use and the improvement of personal functioning.

The book suggests solutions for dealing with clinical challenges in addiction populations, including therapeutic alliance, grounded in humanistic psychology, which is a basic condition for treatment success. It emphasizes emotional passivity, identifying unprocessed emotions, and processing troubling feelings that hinder the creation of interpersonal connections (Timulak & Mcelvaney, 2018); emotional regulation through techniques such as mindfulness and guided imagery, helping bring turbulent emotions to a proportionate level (Elliot et al., 2004); ways of reframing traumatic experiences from a safe perspective, creating an alternative view of the events (Greenberg & Watson, 2006); and processing unclear feelings and unmet emotional needs through imagined dialogues with significant figures (Safean & Muran, 2000). In populations with comorbid addiction and mental health issues, emotional therapy integrated with supportive psychological interventions is required. Focusing on unmet emotional needs, along with actions that promote emotional balance, can help in coping and rehabilitation (Greenberg, 2015; Timulak & Mcelvaney, 2018). The patients' ability to create change in their lives depends on the combination of Emotion-Focused Therapy and instrumental support, which manifests in day-to-day life in promoting problem-solving within the family, housing arrangements, employment rehabilitation, and rights advocacy. These practical interventions can significantly strengthen the patient's sense of self-efficacy and control over their life.

I hope this work sheds light on the unique features of Emotion-Focused Therapy as a meaningful tool for emotional and behavioral change, enabling individuals struggling with addiction to acquire the language of emotional and behavioral change (Miller & Rollnick, 2013; Greenberg & Watson, 2006; Shabi, 2022). This therapy is designed to provide patients with the opportunity to experience positive emotions and mental well-being (Sheldon & Lyubomirsky, 2006), gradually reduce feelings of anxiety and depression (Bolier et al., 2013; Ruini & Fava, 2009), build personal resilience (Peterson & Seligman, 2004), and increase feelings of optimism (Peterson et al., 2012). At the same time, the therapy aims to reduce dependence on psychoactive substances and allow for the experience of recovery and rehabilitation (Shabi, 2022). The Emotion-Focused Therapy approach is characterized by non-judgmental support, compassion, containment, and unconditional support. It provides assistance to people bravely facing significant difficulties and obstacles, creating hope for a better future.

In a concluding therapeutic session, the therapist spoke with a patient who had successfully completed a three-year addiction treatment process, focusing on emotional motivation and emotional change. Throughout the therapy, the patient succeeded in completely stopping alcohol consumption, developed self-confidence, and experienced a sense of control over their life.

"In the time we've spent together," the therapist says, "especially in the last year, I saw self-belief and a sincere desire to change your life. I want to tell you that at a certain point in therapy, I felt how your expectations of yourself, the therapy process, and our relationship became more and more positive.

"Throughout these three years, you maintained an impressive treatment continuity, almost without missing appointments. Today, I see how aware you are of the difficult emotions you've experienced in the past, open to addressing them honestly, and most importantly – managing to change them. You don't just see the difficulty – you confront it and transform it into feelings of capability and control.

"You went through a steady, though gradual, process to reduce your alcohol consumption, until you ultimately decided to quit completely, and succeeded. The last year was full of achievements: following couple's therapy, you improved your relationship with your partner. You returned to working in the construction field, where you had been employed in the past, and you're doing well. This sense of stability and pride is one of the most important outcomes of the work you've done.

"I feel your anxiety about the end of treatment and the independent life awaiting you. Your fears are understandable – will you be able to maintain your achievements? Will you be able to resolve the remaining issues with your family and the community around you? These feelings are legitimate, and I hope that in our last three sessions, we were able to process some of them.

"I am here for you in the future if you need advice or help. What's important for you to remember is that you have made a significant correction in your life. You can be proud of the journey you've taken – from coping with the difficulty to a fundamental change in your lifestyle. I believe in you and in your ability to overcome any obstacle. I believe you will have a good life."

"If I can listen to what the patient is telling me, if I can understand how they experience things, if I can grasp the personal meaning of what they are experiencing and saying, as they understand it, I can promote the change forces within the person" (Carl Rogers)

BIBLIOGRAPHY

Addiction Treatment Service (2020). Annual report 2020. Ministry of Welfare and Social Services. Israel.

Aharonovich, E., Hasin, S., Nunes, E., Stohl, M., Cannizzaro, D., Sarvet, A., Bolla, K., Carroll, K & Genece, K (2018). "Modified Cognitive Behavioral Therapy (M-CBT) for Cocaine Dependence: Development of Treatment for Cognitively Impaired Users and Results from a Stage 1 Trial". *Psychology of Addictive Behaviors, 32*(7), 800–811.

Agosta, L. (2010). *Empathy in the Context of Philosophy*. Palgrave Macmillan.

Agosta, L. (2015). *A Rumor of Empathy: Resistance, Narrative, and Recovery*. Routledge.

Agosta, L. (2018). *Empathy Lessons*. Two Pears Press.

Agosta, L. (2020). "Empathy in cyberspace: The genie is out of the bottle". In H. Weinberg & A. Rolnick, (Eds.), *Theory and practice of online therapy: Internet-delivered interventions for individuals, groups, families, and organizations* (pp. 34–46). Routledge.

Agar, G. (2019). "The clinic offers no advantage over the screen, for relationship is everything, video psychotherapy and its dynamics". In H. Weinberg, & A. Rolnick (1st Eds.), *Theory and Practice of Online Therapy* (pp. 66–78). Routledge. eBook ISBN9781315545530.

American Psycological Association (2017). *Resolution on self – help support groups*. The society for Community Research and Action (APA) Division. Retrieved from http://www.scra27.org/what-we-do/policy/rapid-response-actions/resolution-self-help-support-groups.

Angus, L., Watson, J. C., Elliott, R., Schneider, K., & Timulak, L. (2015). "Humanistic psychotherapy research 1990–2015: From methodological innovation to evidence supported treatment outcomes and beyond". *Psychotherapy Research, 25*(3), 330–347.

Angus, L. E., & Greenberg, L. S. (2011). *Working with narrative in emotion-focused therapy: Changing stories, healing lives*. American Psychological Association.

Apodaca, T. R., Jackson, K. M., Borsari, B. B., Magill, M., Mastroleo, N. R., & Barnett, N. P. (2015). "Which therapist micro-skills elicit client change talk and sustain talk in motivational interviewing?". *Journal of Substance Abuse Treatment, 81*(1), 35–46.

Azrachi, Y., & Harel-Fish, Y. (2017). T*he use of psychoactive substances among the adult population in Israel: The national epidemiological study for the year 2016. National Authority for the War on Drugs and Alcohol.* Israel.

Bandura, A., Freeman, W. H., & Lghtsey, R. (1999). "Self-Efficacy: The exercise of control". *Journal of Cognitive Psychotherapy, 13* (2). 158–166.

Beck, J. S. (2011). *Cognitive Behavior therapy: Basics and Beyond*. The Guilford Press.

Bolier, L., Haverman, M., Westerhof, G. J., Riper, H., Smit, F., & Bohlmeijer, E. (2013). "Positive psychology interventions: A meta-analysis of randomized controlled studies". *BMC Public Health 13* (1), 1–20.

Bowlby, J. (1988). *A secure base*. Basic Books.

Brubacher, L. (2017). "Emotionally focused individual therapy: An attachment-based experiential systemic perspective". *Person-Centered and Experiential Psychotherapies 16*(1), 5.

Brubacher, L. L., & Wiebe, S. A. (2019). "Process-research to practice in Emotionally Focused Couple Therapy: A map for reflective practice". *Journal of Family Psychotherapy, 30* (4), 292–313.

Busfield, J. (2017). "The concept of medicalization reassessed". *Sociology of Health & Illness, 39*(5), 759–774.

Calado, F., & Griffiths, M. D. (2016). "Problem gambling worldwide: An update and systematic review of empirical research (2000–2015)". *Journal of behavioral addictions, 5* (4), 592-613.

Cassidy, J., & Shaver, P. R. (Eds.) (2016). *Handbook of attachment: Theory, research, and clinical applications* (3rd ed.). Guilford.

Center for substance abuse Treatment – CSAT. (2004). *Substance abuse treatment and family therapy (Treatment Improvement Protocol (TIP) Series No. 39, DHHS Publication No. (SMA) 04-3957).* Substance Abuse and Mental Health Services Administration.

Chen, G. (2012). "Social support, spiritual programs, and recovery from addiction to psychoactive substances." In Ronal, N. (Ed.), *Gone with the Wind – Treatment according to the 12-step program* (pp. 27–48). Bar-Ilan University Press. Israel.

Cournoyer, L-G., Brochu, S., Landy, M., & Bergron, J. (2007). "Therapeutic alliance, patient behavior and dropout in a drug rehabilitation program: the moderating effect of clinical subpopulations". *Addiction, 102,* 1960–1970.

Connors, G, J., Diclemente, C. C., Velasques, M. M., & Donovan, D. M. (2013). *Substance abuse treatment and the stages of change: Selecting and planning interventions* (2nd ed.). Guilford Press.

Degnan, A., Seymour- Hyde, Harris, A., & Berry, K. (2014). "The role of therapist attachment in alliance and outcome: A systematic literature review". *Clinical Psychology and Psychotherapy, 23*(1), 47–65.

De Leon, G. (2010). "The therapeutic community: A recovery oriented treatment pathway and the emergence of a recovery-oriented integrated system". In R. Yates, M. S. Malloch (Eds.), *Tackling addiction: Pathways to recovery* (pp. 70-83). Jessica Kingsley Publishers.

American Psychiatric Association. (2013). *Diagnostic and statistical manual of mental disorders* (5th ed.). American Psychiatric Publishing.

Dunn, R., Callahan, J. L., Swift, J. K., & Ivanovic, M. (2013). "Effects of pre-session centering for therapists on session presence and effectiveness". *Psychotherapy Research: Journal of the Society for Psychotherapy Research, 23*(1), 78–85.

Ehlers, A., & Clark, D. M. (2000). "A cognitive model of posttraumatic stress disorder". *Behavior research and therapy, 38*(4), 319-345.

Elliott, R., Watson, J. C., Goldman, R. N., & Greenberg, L. S. (2004). *Learning emotion-focused therapy: The process-experiential approach to change*. American Psychological Association.

Elliott, R., Watson, J. C., Goldman, R. N., & Greenberg, L. S. (2018). *Learning emotion focused therapy: The process-experiential approach to change*. American Psychological Association.

Ettner, S. L., Huang, D., Evans, E., Ash, D. R., Hardy, M., Jourabchi, M., & Hser, Y. I. (2006). "Benefit-cost in the California treatment outcome project: Does substance abuse treatment 'pay for itself'?". *Health Services Research, 41*(1), 192-213.

Flores, P. J. (2004). *Addiction as an attachment disorder*. Aronson.

Furrow, J., Johnson, S. M., Bradley, B., Brubacher, L., Campbell, T. L., Kallos-Lilly, V., Palmer, G., Rheem, K., Woolley, S. (2022). *Becoming an emotionally focused therapist: The workbook* (2nd ed.). Routledge.

Fox, T.P., Oliver, G., & Ellis, S. M. (2013). *The destructive capacity of drug abuse: An Overview exploring the harmful potential of drug abuse both to the individual.* International Scholarly Research Notices.

Gabriel-Fried, B., & Teichman, M. (2008). Self-identity among adolescent children of alcoholics. *Society and Welfare*, 28, 311–328. Israel.

Gabriel-Fried, B. (2023). *Gambling behavior among adolescents*. Mifal HaPais. Israel.

Gabriel-Fried, B., Rehav, G., & Teichman, M. (2010). "Gambling among adolescents in Israel." *Society and Welfare*, 30, 1–24. Israel.

Geller, S. (2020). "Cultivating online therapeutic presence: Strengthening therapeutic relationships in tele therapy sessions". *Counselling Psychology Quarterly*, 1–17.

Gibson, K.E. (2011). *Street kids: Homeless youth, outreach, and policing New York's streets*. New York University Press.

Goldman, R. N., & Greenberg, L. S. (2015). *Case formulation in emotion focused therapy: Co-creating clinical maps for change*. American Psychological Association.

Goldman, R. N., Vaz, A., Rousmaniere, T. (2021). *Deliberate practice in emotion-focused therapy*. American Psychological Association.

Greenberg, L. (2024). *Shame and Anger in Psychotherapy*. The American Psychological Association.

Greenberg, L. S., & Goldman, R. N. (2008). *Emotion-focused couple's therapy: The dynamics of emotion, love, and power*. American Psychological Association.

Greenberg, L. S., & Warwar, S. H. (2006). "Homework in an Emotion-Focused Approach to Experiential Therapy". *Journal of Psychotherapy Integration, 16*(2), 178–200.

Greenberg, L., S. (2010). Emotion focused therapy: A clinical synthesis. *Focus, 8*(1), 32–42.

Greenberg, L. S., & Elliott, R. (2012). Corrective experience from a humanistic– experiential perspective. In L. G. Castonguay, C. E. Hill, L. G. Castonguay, & C. E. Hill (Eds.), *Transformation in psychotherapy: Corrective experiences across cognitive behavioral, humanistic, and psychodynamic approaches* (pp. 85–101). American Psychological Association.

Greenberg, L. S. (2011). Emotion-focused therapy. Washington, D.C.: American Psychological Association.

Greenberg, L. (2015). *Emotion-Focused therapy: coaching client to work through their feeling* (2nd ed.). American Psychological Association.

Greenberg, L. S., & Tomescu, L. R. (2016). *Supervision essentials for emotion-focused therapy*. American Psychological Association.

Greenberg, L. S. (2017). *Emotion-focused therapy: Level 1. Training in emotion focused therapy*. Madrid, Spain.

Greenberg, L. S. (2004). "Emotion–focused therapy". *Clinical Psychology & Psychotherapy, 11*(1), 3-16/10/102qcpp.388.

Greenberg, L. S., Rice, L. N., & Elliott, R. (1996). *Facilitating emotional change: The moment-by-moment process* (1st ed.). The Guilford Press.

Greenberg, L. S., & Safran, J. D. (1987). *Emotion in psychotherapy: Affect, cognition, and the process of change*. Guilford Press.

Greenberg, L. S., & Watson, J. (2006). *Emotion-focused therapy for depression*. American Psychological Association.

Greenman, P., & Johnson, S. (2013). "Process research on EFT for couples: Linking theory to practice". *Family Process, Special Issue: Couple Therapy, 52*(1), 46–61.

Greenman, P., & Johnson, S. M. (2022). "Emotionally focused therapy (EFT): Attachment, connection, and health". *Current Opinion in Psychology, 43*, 146–150.

Gur, A. (2008). "Women addicted to drugs." In H. Mahal, M. Chovav, & M. Golan (Eds.), *Addictions, Violence, and Sexual Offenses* (pp. 93–117). Carmel. Israel.

Hettema, J. (Producer), & Langdon, L. (Director). (2009). *Motivational interviewing training video: Instructional information and demonstrative clinical vignettes, a tool for learners*. Langdon Productions.

Hohman, M. (2012). *Motivational interviewing in social work practice*. Guilford Press.

Ichot, T. I. & Smock, P (2009). *Solution-focused substance abuse treatment*. Taylor & Francis Group, LLC.

Israeli Center for Addictions. (2022). *Report of the Israeli Center for Addictions*. Israel.

Israeli Center for Addictions. (2023). *Survey of the Israeli Center for Addictions*. Israel.

Jacobs, T.J. (2013). *The Possible Profession*. Routledge.

Johnson S. M. (2009). Attachment theory and emotionally focused therapy for individuals and couples. In J. H. Obegi & E. Berant (Eds.), *Attachment theory and research in clinical work with adults* (pp. 410–433). Guilford Press.

Johnson, S. M. (2019). *Attachment theory in practice: Emotionally focused therapy with individuals, couples and families*. Guilford.

Johnson, S. M. (2020). *The practice of emotionally focused therapy: Creating connection (3rd ed.). Routledge.*

Keogh, D., Timulak, L., & McElvaney, J. (2014, June). *Treating generalised anxiety disorder with emotion focused therapy: A case study investigation of emotional change processes*. Annual conference of the Society for Psychotherapy Research.

Khantzian, E. J. (2013). Addiction as a self-regulation disorder and the role of self-medication. *Addiction, 108*(4), 668-669.

Klein, M. H., Mathieu-Coughlan, P., & Kiesler, D. J. (1986). "The experiencing scales". In L. S. Greenberg & W. M. Pinsof (Eds.), *The psychotherapeutic process: A research handbook* (pp. 21–71). Guilford.

Kocsis, B. J., & Yellowlees, P. (2018). "Tele psychotherapy and the therapeutic relationship: Principles, advantages, and case examples". *Telemedicine and e-Health, 24*(5), 329–334.

Kohut, H. (1982). "Introspection, Empathy, and the Semi-circle of Mental Health". *Int. J. of Psycho-Anal, 63,* 395–407.

Lafrance, A., Henderson, K. A., & Mayman, S. (2020). *Emotion focused family therapy: A transdiagnostic model for caregiver-focused interventions. In Emotion focused family therapy: A trans diagnostic model for caregiver-focused interventions*. American Psychological Association.

Lesieur, H. R., & Blume, S. B. (1987). "The South Oaks gambling screen (SOGS): A new instrument for the identification of pathological gamblers". *American Journal of Psychiatry, 144*(1), 1884–1888.

Lev-Ran S., Nitzan U. & Fennig, S (2014). "Examining the ethical boundaries of harm reduction: from addictions to general psychiatry". *Israeli Journal of Psychiatry and Related Sciences, 51*(3), 175–180.

Locke, E. A., & Schattke, K. (2018). "Intrinsic and extrinsic motivation: Time for expansion and clarification". *Motivation Science, 5*(4), 277–290.

Loue, S. (2002). *Diversity Issues in Substance Abuse Treatment and Research.* Academic Publishers New York.

Magill, M., Bernstein, M. H., Hoadley, A., Borsari, B., Apodaca, T. R., Gaume, J., & Tonigan, J. S. (2018). "Do what you say and say what you are going to do: A preliminary meta-analysis of client change and sustain talk subtypes in motivational interviewing". *Psychotherapy Research, 29*(7), 860–869.

Marom, T., Shachtman, A., Mor, M., & Myers, Y. (2011). Cognitive-behavioral therapy in adults. *Dyunon*. Israel.

Mata, G. (2021). *In the Kingdom of Hungry Spirits: Close Encounters with Addiction*. Asia.

McFarlane, A. C., and R. Yehuda. (1996). "Resilience, vulnerability, and the course of posttraumatic reactions". *In* B. A. van der Kolk, A. C. McFarlane, and L. Weisaeth (Eds.), *Traumatic Stress: The Effects of Overwhelming Experience on Mind, Body and Society*. Guilford Press.

McGuinty, E., Nelson, J., Carlson, A., Crowther, E., Bednar, D., & Foroughe, M. (2016). "Redefining outcome measurement: A model for brief psychotherapy: Redefining outcome measurement". *Clinical Psychology & Psychotherapy, 23*(3), 260–271.

McLellan, A. T., Kushner, H., Metzger, D., Peters, R., Smith, I., Grissom, G., Pettinati, H., & Argeriou, M. (1992). "The fifth edition of the Addiction Severity Index". *Journal of Substance Abuse Treatment, 9* (3), 199–213.

Mifal HaPais Survey (2018). *Retrieved in January 2019*: https://www.pais.co.il/specials/responsiblelottery/content.html. Israel.

Mignonn, S, I. (2014). *Substance Abuse Treatment: Options, Challenges, and Effectiveness*. Springer Publishing Company.

Miller, W. R., & Moyers, T. (2017). *Advanced workshop in motivational interviewing*. Workshop attended in Albuquerque, NM, United States.

Miller, W. R., & Rollnick, S. (2002). *Motivational interviewing: Preparing people for change* (2nd ed.). Guilford.

Miller, W. R., & Rollnick, S. (2013). *Motivational interviewing: Helping people change* (3rd. ed.). Guilford.

Maibom, H. L. (2012). "The many faces of empathy and their relation to prosocial action and aggression inhibition". *WIREs Cog Sci 3*, 253–263.

Meier, P. S., Donmall, M. C., Barrowclough, C., McElduff, P., & Heller, R. F. (2005). "Predicting the early therapeutic alliance in the treatment of drug misuse". *Addiction, 100*(4), 500–511.

Ministry of Welfare (2019). People on the continuum of drug, alcohol, and gambling use. *Ministry of Welfare and Social Services*. Israel.

Monezi, A. L. & De Micheli, A. D. (2016). *Innovations in the Treatment of Substance Addiction*. Springer International Publishing.

Naar, S., & Safren, S. A. (2017). *Motivational interviewing and CBT: Combining strategies for maximum effectiveness*. Guilford Press.

Najavits, L.M. (2004). "Assessment of trauma, PTSD, and substance use disorder: A practical guide". In J.P. Wilson & T.M. Keane (Eds.), *Assessing psychological trauma and PTSD* (pp. 466–491). Guilford Press.

Najavits LM. (2002). "Clinicians' views on treating posttraumatic stress disorder and substance use disorder". *J Subst Abuse Treat 22*, 79–85.

Najavits LM, Schm itz M, G o tthardt S, Weiss RD. (2005). "Seeking Safety plus Exposure Therapy: An outcome study on dual diagnosis men". *J Psychoactive Drugs, 37*, 425–435.

National Authority for Community Safety. (2021). *The Icelandic model*. National Authority for Community Safety. Israel.

National Institute on Drug Abuse (NIDA). (2018). *Principles of drug addic-*

tion treatment: A research-based guide. (NIH Publication No. 12–4180). Rockville, MD: National Institutes of Health, U.S. Department of Health and Human Services.

NIDA (2014). *Principles of drug abuse treatment for criminal justice populations – A research-based guide principle.* https://www.drugabuse.gov/publications/principles-drug-abuse-treatment-criminal-justice-populations-research-based-guide/principles.

Oxley, J. C. (2011). *The moral dimensions of empathy: Limits and applications in ethical theory and practice.* Palgrave Macmillan.

Peterson, C., & Seligman, M. E. (2004). "Character strengths and virtues: A handbook and classification". Oxford University Press.

Peterson, C., Park, N., & Kim, E. S. (2012). "Can optimism decrease the risk of illness and disease among the elderly?". *Aging Health, 8*(1), 5–8. doi:10.2217/ahe.11.81.

Petry, N. M., Blanco, C., Stinchfield, R., & Volberg, R. (2013). "An empirical evaluation of proposed changes for gambling diagnosis in the DSM-5". *Addiction, 108,* 575–581.

Pressman, S. D., Kraft, T. L., & Cross, M. P. (2015). "It's good to do good and receive good: The impact of a 'pay it forward' style kindness intervention on giver and receiver well-being". *The Journal of Positive Psychology, 10*(4), 293–302.

Prochaska, J. O., Diclelemene, C. C., & Norcross, J. C. (1992). "In search of how people change: Applications to addictive behaviors". *American Psychologist, 47,* 1102–1114.

Pugh, M., Bell, T., & Dixon, A. (2020). "Delivering tele-chair work: A qualitative survey of expert therapists". *Psychotherapy Research,* 1–16.

Rathgeber, M., Bürkner, P., Schiller, E., & Holling, H. (2019). "The efficacy of emotionally focused couple's therapy and behavioral couple's therapy: A meta-analysis". *Journal of Marital and Family, 45*(3), 447–463.

Rath, T. (2015). *The only type of motivation that leads to success.* Fast Company. Retrieved from www.fastcompany.com/3047370/the-only-type-of-motivation that-leads-to-success.

Reid, A. G. (2016). "Substance use disorders". *Medicine, 44*(12), 701–705.

Rogers, C. (1995). *On becoming a person.* Mariner Books.

Rogers, C. R. (1951). *Client – centered therapy.* Constable.

Rogers, C. R. (1957). "The necessary and sufficed condition of therapeutic personality change". *Journal of counseling psychology, 21,* 95–100.

Rogers, C. R. (1962). "The interpersonal relationships: the core of guidance". *Harvard Educational Review, 32*(4), 416–429.

Rogers, C. R. (1961). *On becoming a person*. London. Constable.

Ronzitti, S., Soldini, E., Smith, N., Clerici, M. & Bowden – Jnes, H (2017). "Gambling Disorder: Exploring Pre-treatment and In-treatment Dropout Predictors. A UK Study". *J Gamble Study, 33*, 1277–1292.

Rosengren, D. B. (2018). *Building motivational interviewing skills: A practitioner workbook* (2nd ed.). Guilford Press.

Rozin, P., Lowery, L., Imada, S., & Haidt, J. (1999). "The CAD triad hypothesis: A mapping between three immoral emotions (contempt, anger, disgust) and three moral codes (community, autonomy, divinity)". *Journal of Personality and social Psychology, 76*, 574–586.

Ruini, C., & Fava, G. A. (2009). Well-being therapy for generalized anxiety disorder. *Journal of Clinical Psychology, 65*(5), 510–519.

Safran, J. D., & Muran, J. C. (2000). *Negotiating the therapeutic alliance: A relational treatment guide*. Guilford Press.

SAMHSA (2013). *TIP 44: Substance abuse treatment for adults in the criminal justice system*.

Sanders, M. (2000). "Community-based parenting and family support interventions and the prevention of drug abuse". *Addictive Behaviors, 25*, 929–942.

Shabi, A. (2024). Patients' perceptions of interpersonal emotion-focused therapy in addiction treatment. *Academic Journal Keshet*. Israel.

Shabi, A. (2023). Resistance, ambivalence, and change: People with drug and alcohol addiction. *Journal of addiction & addictive Disorders*.

Shabi, A. (2021). *The Impact of a Therapeutic Intervention Program on the Wellbeing and Attachment Patterns of Addicts* (Unpublished doctoral dissertation). University of Iasi – Romania.

Shabi, A. (2022). "Social worker interpersonal therapeutic relationships with clients (ITR): The impact of psychological mechanisms on addiction". *Addiction & Addictive Disorders 9*, 085.

Shaver, P. R., Schachner, D. A., & Mikulincer, M. (2005). "Attachment style, excessive reassurance seeking, relationships processes, and depression". *Journal of Personality and Social Psychology, 31*, 343–359.

Sheldon, K. M., & Lyubomirsky, S. (2006). How to increase and sustain positive emotion: The effects of expressing gratitude and visualizing best possible selves. The Journal of Positive *Psychology, 1*(2), 73–82.

Simpson, S., Richardson, L., Pietrabissa, G., Castelnuovo, G., & Reid, C.

(2021). "Video therapy and therapeutic alliance in the age of COVID-19". *Clinical Psychology & Psychotherapy, 28*(2), 409–421.

Straussner, L. A. (2014). "Practice and policy Issues: The changing Landscape". In Straussner, L. A. (Eds.), *Clinical work with substance abusing Clients* (pp. 539–542). Guilford Press.

Thom, B. (2010), "Women in recovery". In R. Yates & M.S. Malloch (eds.), *Tackling addiction: Pathways to recovery* (pp. 52–69). Jessica Kingsley Publishers.

Timulak, L. & Mcelvaney, J. (2018). *Transforming Generalized anxiety. An Emotion- Focused approach.* Routledge.

Timulak, L. (2015). *Transforming emotional pain in psychotherapy: An emotion-focused approach.* Routledge.

Timulak, L. (2017). *Training in emotion-focused therapy for GAD: Training handouts.* Unpublished manuscript.

Tombs, D.L. (2005). *Introduction to addictive behaviors.* Ach. Israel.

Tudor, K., & Meery, T. (2006). *Dictionary of person centered psychology.* Pccs BOOKS.

UNODCP (2018). *World Drug Report.* United Nations Office on Drugs and Crime.

Van Wamel, A., Van Rooijen, S., & Kroon, H. (2015). "Integrated treatment: The model and European experiences". In G. Dom, & F. Moggi (EDs.), *Co-occurring addictive and psychiatric disorders* (pp. 27–45). Springer.

Wampold, B, E. (2009). *Pharmacology and Treatment of Substance Abuse.* Routledge Taylor & Francis Group.

Wamel, A, V., Lempens, A., Neven, A. (2021). "Integrated treatment of dual disorders in The Netherlands: a qualitative study of client experiences". *Advances in dual diagnosis, 14*(4), 183–197.

Wachtel, P. L. (1993).*Therapeutic Communication: Knowing What to Say When.* Guilford Press.

WHO (2018). *Global status report on alcohol and health 2018.* World Health Organization.

Weinberg, H., & Rolnick, A. (2019). "Introduction". In H. Weinberg, & A. Rolnick (Eds.), *Theory and practice of online therapy* (pp. 1–10). Routledge.

Wiebe, S. A., & Johnson, S. M. (2016). "A review of the research in emotionally focused therapy for couples". *Family Process, 55*(3), 390–407.

Wiers, R. W., Gladwin, T. E., Hofmann, W., Salemink, E., &

Ridderinkhof, K. R. (2013). "Cognitive bias modification and cognitive control training in addiction and related psychopathology: Mechanisms, clinical perspectives, and ways forward". *Clinical Psychological Science, 1,* 192–212.

White W, Popovits R. (2001). *Critical incidents: Ethical issues in the prevention and treatment of addiction* (2nd ed.). J. Bloomington, 111.: Chestnut Health Systems.

WHO. (2010). *The Alcohol, Smoking and Substance. Involvement Screening Test (ASSIST).* World health organization.

Wampold, B, E. (2009). *Pharmacology and Treatment of Substance Abuse.* Routledge Taylor & Francis Group.

Yau, M. Y. H., & Potenza, M. N. (2015). "Gambling disorder and other behavioral addictions: Recognition and treatment". *Harvard Review of Psychiatry, 23*(2), 134.

Yalom, I.D. (2002). *The gift of therapy.* Harper Collins Publishers.

Yalom, I. D., & Leszcz, M. (2019). *The theory and practice of group psychotherapy* (6th ed.). Basic Books.

Zaks, A., & Feld, E. (2005). "Sad heroines: The self-perception of women living with a partner addicted to alcohol." *Society and Welfare,* 25, 204–223. Israel.

Zimmer, R., & Boni-Noah, H. (2014). *Prevention of drug and alcohol use.* Bialik. Israel.

Shagi, S. (2014). "Prevention of psychoactive substance use among children and adolescents: Where is the salutogenic approach leading us?" In R. Zimmer & H. Boni-Nah (Eds.), *Prevention of drug and alcohol use* (pp. 86–97). Bialik. Israel.

Zuckoff, A. (2001). *Motivational interviewing: An empirical-phenomenological study of the interpersonal process and client experience of a counseling style* [Unpublished doctoral dissertation]. Duquesne University.

www.ingramcontent.com/pod-product-compliance
Lightning Source LLC
LaVergne TN
LVHW022207200926
848481LV00006B/1879